PRACTICAL GUIDE TO

BETTER ENGLISH

Level III

Teacher's Guide

AGS®

American Guidance Service, Inc.
Circle Pines, Minnesota 55014-1796
1-800-328-2560

Printed in the United States of America

ISBN 0-7854-1798-2

Product Number 93080

A 0 9 8 7 6 5 4 3 2 1

CONTENTS

AGS Practical Guide to Better English

PROGRAM GOAL

The Practical Guide to Better English program is designed to help high school students and adults gain an awareness of the basic elements of the English language and develop proficiency in all the skills necessary for successful written communication in school and in the workplace.

OBJECTIVES

This new four-level program has the following objectives:

• Develop students' *mastery of essential grammar, usage, and mechanics skills* through focused instruction and practice.

• Build students' *vocabulary and store of background knowledge* through the use of informative, interesting real-world content.

• Improve students' *writing skills at the sentence, paragraph, and whole-composition levels* through the use of accessible models and directed practice in the various writing domains.

• Build students' *self-sufficiency in revising and proofreading* by providing a complete Handbook of grammar, usage, and mechanics rules bound into each pupil book. Students can use this as a resource when they revise written work in other classes and outside school.

Levels I–IV
Scope and Sequence of Grammar, Usage, and Mechanics Skills

	LEVEL			
	I	II	III	IV
CAPITALIZATION				
Capitalize first word in sentence	•	•	•	•
Capitalize proper nouns	•	•	•	•
Capitalize proper adjectives	•	•	•	•
Capitalize days of week	•	•	•	•
Capitalize months NOT seasons	•	•	•	•
Capitalize holidays, festivals	•	•	•	•
Capitalize the word *I*	•	•	•	•
CAPITALIZATION WITH PUNCTUATION				
Capitalize initial; use period	•	•	•	•
Capitalize personal title; use period	•	•	•	•
Capitalize abbreviations of day, week, month; use period		•	•	•
Capitals in addresses, punctuation	•	•	•	•
Commas in address in sentence	•	•	•	•
Capitalize words in titles	•	•	•	•
Draw line under title of book, movie	•	•	•	•
Quotation marks around title of poem, story	•	•	•	•
Direct vs. indirect quotations		•	•	•
Punctuate direct quotations	•	•	•	•
Commas in direct quotations	•	•	•	•
End punctuation in direct quotations	•	•	•	•
Quote inside quote: single quotation marks			•	
OTHER USES OF COMMAS				
Comma in date (or no)	•	•	•	•
Comma after day, year	•	•	•	•
Comma after name, direct address	•	•	•	•
Comma after introductory word	•	•	•	•
Commas to set off interrupting word				•
Comma in compound sentence	•	•	•	•
Comma after introductory dependent clause		•	•	•
Commas to set off nonrestrictive clauses				•
Commas in series	•	•	•	•
Comma to separate adjectives				•
Appositive			•	•
Commas to set off appositive			•	•
PARTS OF SPEECH				
Nouns	•	•	•	•
Proper nouns	•	•	•	•
Nouns—singular and plural	•	•	•	•

	LEVEL			
	I	II	III	IV
Plural: most add -*s*	•	•	•	•
Plural with *ch, sh, s, x, z*	•	•	•	•
Plural with *f* or *fe*	•	•	•	•
Plural with consonant + *y*	•	•	•	•
Plural with vowel + *y*	•	•	•	•
Plurals: irregular	•	•	•	•
Some plurals same as singular	•	•	•	•
Possessive nouns		•	•	•
Possessive nouns: form singular with *'s*	•	•	•	•
Possessive nouns: plural ending in -*s* and NOT ending in -*s*			•	•
Pronouns: personal	•	•	•	•
Pronouns: subject	•	•	•	•
Pronouns: as direct object	•	•	•	•
Pronouns: object of preposition	•	•	•	•
Pronouns: *I* or *me* last in pair or series	•	•	•	•
Pronouns preceding nouns		•	•	•
Pronouns: compound personal		•	•	•
Pronouns: interrogative			•	•
Pronouns: demonstrative			•	•
Verbs: action, being	•	•	•	•
Verb phrase; helping verbs		•	•	•
Agreement in number	•	•	•	•
Agreement: *you are/were*		•	•	•
Agreement: *there is/are*	•	•	•	•
Agreement: compound subjects with *and/or*		•	•	•
Verbs: principal parts	•	•	•	•
First principal part		•	•	•
Second principal part		•	•	•
Third principal part		•	•	•
Present participle			•	•
Second and third principal parts sometimes the same			•	•
Simple verb tenses: past, present, future			•	•
Perfect tenses			•	•
Contractions	•	•	•	•
Adjectives	•	•	•	•
Articles (*an* before vowel)	•	•	•	•
Adjectives: demonstrative			•	•
Possessives act as adjectives			•	•
Use adjective (not adverb) as predicate adjective			•	•

Scope and Sequence of Grammar, Usage, and Mechanics Skills

Skill	I	II	III	IV
Adjectives: comparative/superlative	•		•	•
Adverbs	•	•	•	
Adverbs modify verbs	•	•	•	
Adverbs modify adjectives			•	•
Adverbs modify adverbs			•	•
Don't confuse adverbs and adjectives			•	•
Adverbs: comparative/superlative				•
Prepositions	•	•	•	
Prepositional phrases/elements		•	•	•
Prepositional phrases: adjectival			•	•
Prepositional phrases: adverbial			•	•
Prepositions: pairs with different meanings		•	•	•
Conjunctions: coordinating		•	•	•
Conjunctions: subordinating		•	•	•
Combining sentences	•	•	•	•
Interjections			•	•
VERBALS				
Verbals				•
Participle/participial phrase				•
Infinitive/infinitive phrase				•
Gerund/gerund phrase				•
TROUBLESOME VERBS				
Teach vs. *learn*	•	•	•	•
May vs. *can*	•	•	•	•
Sit vs. *set*	•	•	•	•
Lie (verb)		•	•	•
Lay (verb)		•	•	•
WORD STUDY				
Synonyms	•	•	•	•
Prepositional phrase used instead of a single word			•	•
Antonyms	•	•	•	•
Unnecessary words, eliminating	•	•	•	•
Negatives	•	•	•	•
Unsuitable expressions, eliminating	•	•	•	•
Homophones	•	•	•	•
SENTENCES				
Sentence/fragment/run-on/comma splice	•	•	•	•
Sentence: declarative	•	•	•	•
Sentence: interrogative	•	•	•	•

Skill	I	II	III	IV
Sentence: imperative			•	•
Sentence: exclamatory	•	•	•	•
Subject/predicate—simple subject	•	•	•	•
Compound subject		•	•	•
Complete subject		•	•	•
Simple predicate	•	•	•	•
Compound predicate		•	•	•
Complete predicate		•	•	•
Subject or predicate, difficult to identify			•	•
Direct object/compound direct object		•	•	•
Indirect object			•	•
Object pronouns as indirect/direct objects			•	•
Predicate noun/predicate adjective		•	•	•
Simple sentence	•	•	•	•
Compound sentence	•	•	•	•
Complex sentence/dependent clause				•
Adjective clause				•
Adverb clause				•
PARAGRAPHS				
Paragraphs and compositions	•	•	•	•
Suggestions for writing a paragraph	•	•	•	•
LETTERS				
Friendly letter: parts	•	•	•	•
Friendly letter: capitalization/punctuation	•	•	•	•
Business letter: parts	•	•	•	•
Business letter: greeting/close/signature		•	•	•
Business letter: capitalization/punctuation/postal codes	•	•	•	•
Envelope	•	•	•	•
USING A DICTIONARY				
Dictionary: introduction	•	•	•	•
Dictionary: alphabetical order	•	•	•	•
Syllables	•	•	•	•
Word division—introduction	•	•	•	•
Word division—rules			•	•
Respelling for pronunciation		•	•	•
Spelling		•	•	•
SPEAKING AND LISTENING				
Speaking	•	•	•	•
Listening	•	•	•	•

Student Book Organization

The *Practical Guide to Better English* **Student Book** for each level includes the following elements and features:

INSTRUCTION

- 72 one-page grammar/usage/mechanics *instructional lessons*—nine per unit.
- 8 two-page *composition lessons*—one per unit.
- 8 one-page grammar/usage/mechanics *unit reviews*—one per unit.

CUMULATIVE REVIEW

- A year-end review unit consisting of 9 one-page grammar/usage/mechanics *review lessons* and a final two-page *cumulative review.*

HANDBOOK RESOURCE

- A *Handbook of grammar, usage, and mechanics rules* organized topically into 54 Guides.
- *Practice activities* following each Handbook section, for each principle explained in the Handbook.

Each lesson directs students to the appropriate Guide or Guides in the Handbook for explicit instruction in grammar, usage, and mechanics principles. In addition, an alphabetical index to topics covered in the Handbook is included at the end of the book.

WORD STUDY

- *Vocabulary puzzlers* of various kinds build students' knowledge of word structure, word meanings, and word relationships.

CORRELATION OF HANDBOOK GUIDES TO LESSONS

HANDBOOK GUIDE	LESSONS
1 Capitalization	6, 9, 11, 30, 33, 50, 63, 74, 88, 96
Capitalization/Punctuation	
2 Initials of Names	9, 74, 88, 96
3 Titles with Names	9, 30, 74, 88, 96
4 Abbreviations	88
5 Addresses	88
6 Addresses in Sentences	30, 33, 50, 66, 74
7 Titles	9, 11, 32, 63, 96
8 Quotations	31, 33, 50, 63, 74, 79, 96
Other Uses of Commas	
9 Dates	30, 66, 74
10 Direct Address	8, 11, 50, 74
11 Introductory Words	8, 11, 30, 33, 63, 74, 96
12 Words in Series/	
Compound Sentences	8, 11, 30, 50, 63, 74, 96
13 Appositives	8, 11, 50, 63, 74, 96, 98
Parts of Speech	
14 Nouns	6, 11, 81
15 Singular & Plural Forms	7, 91
16 Possessive Forms	16, 22, 38, 44, 74, 86, 91, 96
17 Pronouns	17, 24, 26, 27, 29, 41, 45, 52, 55, 64, 81, 86, 87, 91
18 Compound Personal	
Pronouns	28, 33, 41, 52, 86, 91
19 Interrogative Pronouns	28, 33, 52, 91
20 Demonstrative Pronouns	28, 33
21 Verbs	13, 23, 25, 34, 81, 92
22 Verb Phrases	13, 23, 25, 34, 55, 92
23 Singular & Plural Forms	14, 15, 22, 71, 72, 75, 86
24 Principal Parts	20, 22, 42, 53, 64, 68, 69, 70, 75, 77, 86, 92, 98
25 Adjectives	10, 37, 38, 39, 44, 45, 52, 55, 61, 64, 65, 66, 76, 81, 83, 86, 93, 98
26 Adverbs	46, 47, 48, 49, 55, 61, 64, 66, 76, 81, 86, 93
27 Prepositions	26, 29, 33, 56, 57, 58, 59, 64, 65, 66, 81, 86, 94, 98
28 Conjunctions	67, 76, 77, 81, 98
29 Interjections	67, 77, 81
30 Contractions	16, 30, 33, 45, 52, 55, 74, 86, 96, 98
Troublesome Verbs	
31 *Teach* and *Learn*	53, 55, 97
32 *May* and *Can*	53, 55, 97
33 *Sit* and *Set*	53, 55, 86, 97
34 *Lie* and *Lay*	40, 44, 53, 64, 86, 97
Word Study	
35 Synonyms	78
36 Prepositional Phrases	56, 57
37 Antonyms	78
38 Unnecessary Words	51, 60, 64, 86, 97
39 Double Negatives	60, 64, 86, 97
40 Expressions to Be	
Avoided	53, 60, 64, 86
41 Homophones	80
Sentences	
42 Fragments & Run-ons	1, 73, 89
43 Kinds of Sentences	2, 11, 30, 33, 50, 89
44 Sentence Elements:	
Subject & Predicate	3, 4, 5, 11, 12, 18, 19, 22, 25, 34, 82, 90
45 Direct Object/Predicate	
Noun, Adjective	23, 24, 25, 27, 29, 33, 34, 62, 82, 90
46 Sentence Structure	63, 77
47 Paragraphs	10, 21, 32, 39, 43, 54, 65, 76, 87
48 Business Letters	84, 88, 95
Using a Dictionary	
49 Uses	36, 85
50 Alphabetical Order	35, 85
51 Syllables	35, 36, 44
52 Pronunciation	36
53 Spelling	36
54 Speaking & Listening	(Oral language development is supported throughout lessons.)

Teacher's Guide Organization

The *Practical Guide to Better English* **Teacher's Guide** for each level includes the following resources for teaching and managing the program:

OVERVIEW
- **Overviews** of the program, the student book, and the teacher's guide.

SCOPE AND SEQUENCE
- **Scope and Sequence Chart** of the grammar, usage, and mechanics skills taught in each level.

CORRELATION
- **Correlation** between the Handbook topics and individual lessons for that level.

PROCEDURES
- A **description of the five-step process of teaching a unit:** administering the diagnostic test; presenting each individual skill lesson; teaching the writing lesson; using the review lesson; and administering the achievement test.

- A **description of the basic sequence for presenting a lesson:** introducing the skill; directing students to the instructional text; previewing the content; assigning the lesson items; checking answers; assigning additional activities; and reviewing the lesson.

- **Suggestions for introducing the program** to students.

- **Descriptions of instructional procedures and options for meeting students' individual needs:** tips for classroom management; for promoting oral language development; for teaching composition; for adapting lessons to meet students' individual needs; and for helping students who are acquiring English.

- **Procedures and materials for evaluation of student progress:** suggested informal and formal assessment methods; reproducible blackline masters of diagnostic and achievement tests for each unit; a reproducible record-keeping form for tracking individual progress; and a rubric and checklists for use in evaluating the writing lessons.

ANSWER KEYS
- **Answer keys** for diagnostic and achievement tests and for student book lessons.

INDEX
- **Index of topical content** of individual lessons in the student book for that level.

How to Teach a Unit

Level III of *Practical Guide to Better English* includes eight instructional units and a final review unit. The units are developmental and are intended to be taught in the order in which they are presented. Nevertheless, it is entirely appropriate to present lessons—or units—in any order that fits with your instructional goals. Each lesson in the program can stand alone because each is fully supported by instructions in the Handbook.

Each unit will take about three weeks to teach. The pace can easily be slowed or accelerated, however, to fit with students' progress.

Practical Guide to Better English
UNIT PLANNER
Option 1: Daily Practice

	MONDAY	TUESDAY	WEDNESDAY	THURSDAY	FRIDAY
Week 1	Diagnostic Test	Lesson 1	Lesson 2	Lesson 3	Lesson 4
Week 2	Lesson 5	Lesson 6	Lesson 7	Lesson 8	Lesson 9
Week 3	Composition Planning and Writing	Composition Revision	Composition Presentation	Review Lesson	Achievement Test

Practical Guide to Better English
UNIT PLANNER
Option 2: Three-Day-a-Week Practice

	MONDAY	TUESDAY	WEDNESDAY	THURSDAY	FRIDAY
Week 1	Diagnostic Test/ Lesson 1		Lesson 2		Lesson 3
Week 2	Lesson 4		Lesson 5		Lesson 6
Week 3	Lesson 7		Lesson 8		Lesson 9
Week 4	Composition Planning and Writing		Composition Revision and Presentation/ Review Lesson		Achievement Test

The recommended procedure for teaching a unit involves these five steps:

1. Administer the diagnostic test.

The diagnostic test for each unit can be used to measure what students know at the *beginning* of a unit. The diagnostic test should be administered before students begin working on the unit skill lessons. Students' performance on a diagnostic test can be compared with their performance on the achievement test, given at the end of the unit. Reproducible masters for the diagnostic tests begin on page 24 of this teacher's guide. A reproducible record-keeping form for the diagnostic and achievement tests is included on page 60.

2. Present each individual skill lesson.

Each unit contains nine skill lessons. It is recommended that one lesson be taught each day. Suggested procedures for presenting a lesson appear in the next section of this teacher's guide. The time required to teach a particular lesson will vary according to the difficulty of the concept, the nature of the practice, the instructional procedures used, and the students' ability.

3. Teach the writing lesson.

Each instructional unit contains a two-page writing lesson following the regular skill lessons. These activities lead students step-by-step through the task of writing and revising original compositions. A writing lesson can be completed in two or three class periods, depending on the available time and the students' writing proficiency. Each writing lesson has been designed so that students can complete it independently; however, some students may need additional guidance. Suggested procedures for presenting the writing lessons appear on pages 18–19 of this teacher's guide. A rubric for evaluating compositions and checklists for scoring the writing lessons can be found on pages 61-65.

4. Assign the review lesson.

A review lesson at the end of each instructional unit briefly covers the skills and concepts taught in the lessons. The review lesson is designed to reinforce learning and also indicate areas in which students may need remediation. Class time remaining after administering and checking the review lesson should be used to provide students with help on the skills they have not fully grasped, which should include careful review of the Handbook sections that instruct those skills.

5. Administer the achievement test.

At the conclusion of each unit, a two-page achievement test should be administered to all students. Reproducible masters for the achievement tests begin on page 26 of this teacher's guide. Students' performance on this test can be compared with their performance on the diagnostic test to measure progress. The reproducible record-keeping form on page 60 of this guide may be used to keep track of student progress. For more information on assessment procedures and options, see "Assessment" on pages 22–23 of this teacher's guide.

How to Present a Lesson

Each unit in Level III of *Practical Guide to Better English* includes nine skill lessons. All lessons have a common structure that allows for as much or as little teacher guidance as a teacher chooses to provide.

The teaching procedure outlined here calls for teacher guidance throughout the lesson. Although it requires more time and direct involvement, this procedure offers a number of benefits: more opportunities for oral language development, effective use of scaffolding, modeling of correct English usage, constructive feedback, and authentic ongoing assessment. This procedure is especially recommended for use in the first few weeks of the school term, and whenever challenging new grammar concepts are being introduced.

If teacher involvement is impractical, students can be directed to complete the skill lessons independently. *All lessons in this program are written to be self-directing.* In addition, the Handbook serves as a dependable source of information for students working on their own. The more students use the Handbook as a resource, the better prepared they will be for success on the job, where the ability to use information in a manual or a handbook is a key to advancement.

Additional suggestions for presenting skill lessons are included in the sections of this teacher's guide that focus on managing classrooms, developing oral language, adapting lessons to meet individual needs, and helping students who are acquiring English.

RECOMMENDED SEQUENCE

1. Introduce the skill. Read the lesson title aloud. Engage students by asking questions that will help them make connections to previous lessons and prior knowledge. For example, for the lesson entitled "Capitalization," you might ask, *"What are some of the types of words that are always capitalized? Which word in a sentence is always capitalized? What are some abbreviations that are capitalized?"*

2. Direct students to the instructional text. Point out the Handbook Guide(s) listed in the gray box. If a rule statement is given in the box, ask a volunteer to read it aloud. Next, have students find the guide(s) in their Handbooks, read the instructional text, complete the practice items, and check their answers. (If the practice items have been completed previously, have students review just the rules and the examples.) Students who are unable to complete the Handbook practice items successfully may need special help before they begin working on the lesson.

3. Preview the content. Discuss with students the lesson topic. This can be determined by skimming the exercise sentences. The "Index of Topics Featured in Level III" at the end of this teacher's guide may also be used to identify the topic. Invite students to share what they already know about the topic. For example, for the lesson that tells about morays, you might ask: *"What are morays? Has anyone seen a moray, or a picture of one? What did it look like? Are morays dangerous? What makes them dangerous? What can swimmers and divers do to keep from being harmed by morays?"* By helping students focus on the content topic and building their background knowledge, you increase the likelihood that they will read the lesson items with good comprehension and become engaged with the language and content of the lesson.

4. Assign the items. Read aloud the instructions. Invite a volunteer to copy the example items on the chalkboard. Read aloud the items, describe how you would decide on the correct response, and model how you would write your response on the board. Then ask students to complete the lesson items independently or with partners.

5. Check answers. Invite volunteers to give their responses to the items orally; have students check their own work. Use the lesson answer key at the end of this teacher's guide to verify that responses given by students are correct. Invite students to ask questions about items they found difficult or confusing.

6. Assign the additional section or vocabulary activity. If the lesson has a Part II activity or a vocabulary puzzler, read aloud the instructions for it and discuss any examples. Next, have students complete the activity independently or with a partner. Then have volunteers give their answers while students check their own work. For those Part II activities that ask students to write original sentences, you may want to evaluate responses yourself.

7. Review the lesson. Have students count their correct responses and record their score at the top of the page and also on the score chart on page 176 of their books. Then invite one student to restate the rules and concepts learned in the lesson and tell how he or she can put these to use in writing and speaking.

Introducing the Program to Students

Teachers report that high school and adult students generally work more productively in courses in which the goals, instructional focus, procedures, and benefits are outlined in advance. Accordingly, you may want to use the following sequence to introduce *Practical Guide to Better English* to students.

1. Preview. Invite students to preview the book and talk about what they notice. Point out the goal statement at the beginning of "A Note to Students," which appears before the Contents page.

2. Set goals. Ask students to suggest reasons why it is important to be able to speak and write effectively using correct English. Record their reasons on the chalkboard. Then suggest to students that they choose one or more of these reasons as their personal goals and write these on a sheet of paper.

3. Look at one lesson. Have students all turn to one instructional lesson, such as Lesson 5, on page 9 of their books. Point out the *lesson title*, which gives the skill focus. Then point out the shaded box with the *listing of Handbook Guides*. Explain that these Handbook Guides have the rules and information they will need to learn in order to complete the lessons. Point out that the box also contains a rule reminder. Next, point out the instructions for the lesson and the examples of how to complete the items. Finally, point out the numbered *lesson items* and the *vocabulary puzzler* entitled "Synonym Watch."

4. Look at the Handbook. Explain to students that the Handbook is a reference they can use to learn and check what is correct English. Remind students that each lesson has a listing of the Handbook Guides they will need to study for that lesson. Have them turn to the Handbook Guides listed for Lesson 5—Guides 44a-f. Have volunteers read aloud the guides and orally complete the practice items. Then point out the answers; explain to students that as they read the guide sections, they should complete the practice items and check their answers to make sure they understand the rules.

5. Model the procedure for completing a lesson independently. Have a volunteer read aloud the steps for completing the lessons on page 2 of the student book. After each step is read, describe how you would carry this out for Lesson 5.

6. Look at one writing lesson. Explain to students that in addition to learning the rules of written English, they will have several opportunities to put the rules into action by writing their own compositions. Inform them that there are eight writing lessons in the book, and that each one teaches a particular kind of writing.

Introduce the writing lessons by having students turn to Lesson 21 of Unit II, "Writing a Biography," on pages 26–27. Point out the *lesson title*. Then point out the bulleted list of *tips*. Explain that each writing lesson has a list of guidelines for the type of writing focused on in the lesson. Direct students' attention to the *writing model* and explain that it is an example of the writing form. As they write their own biography, they can look at the model for help. Finally, point out the heading *Write a Biography* on page 27. Explain that these sections guide them through the steps of planning and writing. Point out that they will write their biography on another piece of paper.

7. Discuss assessment procedures. Explain to students that they will take a test at the beginning and end of each unit. The diagnostic test at the beginning of each unit will indicate what they already know about the skills and rules that will be taught in the unit. The achievement test at the end of each unit will show what they have learned. Then tell students that in addition to the test the following activities will be evaluated: the sentences and paragraphs they write; how well they are able to revise and correct their work; how effectively they speak and listen; and their scores on the instructional lessons and review lessons.

Explain that these assessments can help identify concepts and rules they don't fully understand and skills they have not yet mastered. Assure students that you will work with them to help them master the skills and concepts that initially cause them problems.

Tips for Classroom Management

The *Practical Guide to Better English* program requires minimal teacher direction. As a result, it helps solve classroom management problems rather than create them. *All lessons in the program are self-instructive*, so students can be directed to work independently, or in pairs or small groups, while you work with the rest of the class on another task. The self-instructive nature of the lessons, plus the support for independent learning provided by the Handbook, allow for great flexibility in pacing and grouping, as described in the following sections.

Flexibility. The program provides a year's course of study. Lessons are developmental, and spiral learning occurs within and across levels to reinforce concepts and skills. The program can be easily adapted to suit the needs of individual classrooms because *every skill lesson can stand alone*. The Handbook Guides referenced in each lesson provide students with the concepts and rules they need to complete the lesson successfully. Further, since the Handbook itself is organized in sensible sequence to explain grammar, usage, and mechanics concepts, students who find themselves unsure of how a particular rule fits in the greater fabric of correct English can read the Handbook Guide sections before and after the sections referenced to gain a better understanding.

As you use this level of *Practical Guide to Better English* in your classroom, feel free to expand, drop, or change the order of lessons. Your sense of what will be of greatest value to your students is the best guide to what lessons should be taught when.

Pacing. Because the skill lessons in *Practical Guide to Better English* are self-instructive and free-standing, the program offers more pacing options than comparable programs. Among these options are the following:

- The whole class can proceed at a single pace.

- Students can be grouped heterogeneously, and all groups can proceed at a similar pace.

- Students can be grouped homogeneously, and each group can proceed at a pace appropriate for its members.

- Students who need work on all skills and concepts can work through the program together at a steady pace. Students who have greater proficiency can work on just those lessons that focus on problems that show up in their written work.

- All students can work at their own pace, checking in with you each time they are ready to begin or conclude a unit.

Grouping. Most students will benefit from working with other students at least part of the time. Group work offers opportunities for oral language development, cooperative problem-solving, peer tutoring and counseling, shared reading, and oral presentation of written work to an audience. Each mode offers particular advantages:

- Working in *small heterogeneous groups* allows students with less advanced literacy skills to benefit from the modeling and mentoring of more proficient students. In turn, the more proficient students develop communications skills and strengthen their own knowledge of grammar, usage, and mechanics principles as they work to convey these concepts to others in the group.

- Working in *small homogeneous groups* offers greater opportunities for providing scaffolding. (See "Adapting Lessons to Meet Students' Individual Needs" on pages 20–21 of this teacher's guide.) Many teachers report that students are most comfortable and work most productively in groups in which other students have the same level of proficiency. In part this may be because members of such groups can all contribute to the problem-solving process—none of them has all the answers.

- Working in *pairs* encourages thought and dialogue. Many of the skills activities in the lessons in *Practical Guide to Better English* lend themselves to partnered learning. Pairs of students working on the same lesson can share prior knowledge of the skill and the lesson topic, and read and discuss the Handbook Guides together. They can work independently on the exercise items, and then reconvene to check answers and help each other clear up any areas of confusion.

Promoting Oral Language Development

The process of acquiring English language skills begins with oral language development. Students need to hear correct language patterns, and practice producing these in their own speech, in order to internalize the patterns and employ them in their writing.

Oral communication is of particular benefit to students with limited fluency and knowledge of the English language because it allows them to experiment with language in a setting that is less formal and less threatening than written formats. At the same time, oral language activities—listening as well as speaking—expand students' vocabularies, which is essential for their educational progress and eventual success in the working world.

In order to develop oral language skills, students should have opportunities to do these things:

- Listen and speak for a **variety of purposes**: give directions, seek information, express opinions, respond to requests.

- Listen to and contribute ideas **in various settings**: one-to-one, small-group, and whole-class discussions.

- Listen and speak to share **knowledge about lesson topics.**

- Listen to and read aloud **models of basic grammatical structures** in order to gain oral fluency using proper syntax.

- Listen to and repeat **accurate pronunciation of words** in order to achieve effective oral communication.

- Listen to and discuss the **differences between formal and informal language** and the settings in which each is appropriate.

- Listen to and repeat examples of the **diversity of language** and recognize how it is used for different purposes and audiences in various types of communication.

The instructional skill lessons in *Practical Guide to Better English* offer many opportunities for listening and speaking:

- When a skill lesson is first presented, students can **share knowledge and opinions about the lesson topics.**

- During the lesson introduction, students can **read aloud rule statements, discuss examples, suggest other examples orally, or complete the Handbook practice activities orally.**

- As the class prepares to complete the skill lesson, students can **read aloud the instructions or the lesson sentences.**

- After students complete the lesson, they can **give correct answers orally and explain how they decided that they were correct.**

- Prior to completing open-ended exercise items (writing sentences with a certain grammatical element, combining sentences, and so on), students can **read aloud the items and discuss possible responses to each.**

- If the lesson offers a vocabulary extension activity, students can **solve the vocabulary puzzler orally.**

- As an extension activity, students inspired by the topic of a particular lesson can **prepare and present brief oral reports.**

The writing lessons also offer opportunities for productive oral expression:

- When a writing form is introduced, students can **share what they know** about that form and discuss any writing or reading experiences they may have had with that type of writing.

- Students can **read the writing model aloud** and share their reactions. For instance, after reading a persuasive paragraph, they might give their own opinions about the issue. After reading a science report, they might share other facts they know about the topic.

- Students can **orally answer the questions** that ask them to identify specific elements in the model.

- As they plan their own writing, students can work cooperatively to **brainstorm topic ideas** or **discuss the sequence of ideas** that might work best for expository or narrative compositions.

- Revising written work offers students the opportunity to **give and receive constructive feedback**: students can trade drafts and **offer suggestions** for revision.

- Students can **read aloud their completed writing**; listeners can **give their reactions**.

- Process writing lessons also offer students multiple opportunities for oral expression as they **brainstorm, revise,** and **publish** their work.

Teaching Composition

The writing component of *Practical Guide to Better English* offers students the opportunity to apply grammar, usage, and mechanics skills in the context of original compositions. Authentic writing activities ask students to draw upon their own experiences, opinions, interests, and ideas, as well as factual information from the content areas. They can use these experiences as they learn to construct paragraphs, essays, reports, narratives, and other standard forms of writing required for success in school, on state assessment tests, in daily life, and in the workplace.

The Domains of Writing. The domains of writing are generally (although not universally) identified as **expository, persuasive, narrative,** and **descriptive.** The writing lessons in *Practical Guide to Better English* reflect the writing requirements and domains currently in use in many states across the country. The lessons are designed to help students understand that each form of writing has its own purpose, audience, and structure. The forms listed in the chart below are taught in the *Practical Guide to Better English* writing lessons.

Program Goals. The writing exercises and lessons of *Practical Guide to Better English* are designed to help students develop writing fluency at the sentence, paragraph, and whole composition levels. The program is developmental in nature, beginning with simple tasks and progressing to more challenging ones—both within and across grade levels. The lessons are designed to help students develop these skills:

- Write in a variety of circumstances: in response to questions that require single-sentence answers; to writing prompts that require a response of one or more paragraphs; and to longer, more formal assignments.

- Use the steps of the writing process.

- Revise writing based on feedback and reflection.

- Use the conventions of grammar and spelling, and develop good proofreading habits.

- Write for real-life situations: college or job applications, letters, resumes, and so on.

Process Writing vs. Demand Writing. Of the eight writing lessons presented in each level of *Practical Guide to Better English*, two take students through the steps of the writing process. The other six lessons guide students in developing shorter compositions, what some researchers call *demand writing*. Demand writing requires students to develop a clear, cohesive response to a specific writing prompt, in a controlled setting, often in a limited amount of time. Preparation for statewide writing proficiency tests is one good reason to teach demand writing; another is its wealth of real-life applications. As adults, students will engage in demand writing in most cases when writing is required—when composing letters, filling out job applications, giving directions and explanations, and in many other everyday tasks.

The writing lessons in Units IV and VIII teach students a useful method for developing longer, more complex compositions, such as research reports, essays, and narratives.

EXPOSITORY	PERSUASIVE	NARRATIVE	DESCRIPTIVE
compare/contrast (III)	**persuasive paragraph (I, II)**	**personal narrative (I, II, III)**	descriptive sentences (I)
research report (I, III)	**persuasive essay (IV)**	**story—narrative elements (I, II, IV)**	descriptive paragraph (I, II)
summary (I, III)	product endorsement (III)		descriptive composition (III)
how-to paragraph (I, II)	résumé (IV)		descriptive essay (IV)
problem/solution (II, IV)	**letter of application for employment (IV)**		
paragraph of information (II)			
explanation (II, IV)			
biography (III)			
news articles (III)			

(Assignments that appear in boldface type are presented as process writing activities at least once in the program. Numbers in parentheses indicate at which level[s] the writing form is taught.)

TEACHING THE WRITING LESSONS

Each writing lesson is designed so that students can complete it independently. However, some students may need additional support. Here are some suggestions for adapting the writing lessons for students with differing needs:

Students Acquiring English. In the sequence of language acquisition, writing fluency is usually the last skill second-language learners acquire. When teaching composition to students acquiring English, help them develop ideas and try out sentence structures by offering opportunities for oral language expression before, during, and after writing. (See the section entitled "Promoting Oral Language Development" in this teacher's guide for oral language opportunities in the writing lessons.)

Here are some additional procedures that can help second-language learners:

• **Determine students' writing fluency in their native language.** Ask students to describe writing they have done. Have them describe the processes they use when they write. (Example: *If you wanted to compare a lion and a tiger, how would you do it in writing?*) If students possess writing fluency in their native language, they are likely to need less instruction on the structure of the various writing forms taught in this program.

• **Provide support with syntax.** Students acquiring English are likely to struggle with usage issues such as subject-verb agreement, pronoun use, article use, verb forms, and sentence structure. Have students identify and tag the Handbook Guides that focus on these, and remind them to refer to those sections often. In addition, you may need to assign specific usage lessons a second time.

• **Pair each second-language learner with a partner who is fluent in English.** Have the partner read aloud the writing model, and have the student acquiring English retell it orally. Partners can then discuss the writing assignment together and talk about what they plan to write. The second-language learner can dictate his or her paragraph(s). Partners should work together to proofread and correct their work.

Students with Little or No Writing Experience. Students with limited writing experience often have little idea of how to begin a writing assignment; they also typically do not know what is expected in terms of the product. Group these students *homogeneously* and go through the first several writing assignments with them, modeling how you would complete each step. Then walk students through the lesson again, this time having students complete the various parts of the writing activity as a group. It is particularly important for these students to spend time thinking about how the writing model is structured because they bring little knowledge with them about the organization and purpose of different writing forms. As students gain confidence as writers and familiarity with the various domains, gradually encourage them to tackle the writing lessons in pairs or independently.

Students with Poor Reading Fluency. Some students who are poor readers can be quite successful at writing, with guidance and encouragement. It may benefit these students to complete the writing activities with a *peer partner* who has good reading skills, but may be a less fluent writer or inventive thinker. That student can read the tips, writing model, and instructions aloud, and the partners can help each other plan and write their paragraphs.

Reluctant Writers. Students who display a reluctance to write may be encouraged to begin by writing only a small amount—perhaps just one sentence. You may need to work with these students *individually.* Encourage all efforts, no matter how minimal the outcome may seem: one sentence is a beginning! Gradually, encourage students to add sentences until they are composing complete paragraphs. Alternately, you might put off teaching the writing lessons until later in the year, when students' writing fluency at the sentence level has increased and their confidence as writers has improved.

Special Help for Nonproductive Writers. Students who possess little writing fluency frequently feel intimidated by even simple writing tasks, and often bring with them years of frustration and discouragement. Here are some additional suggestions for helping these students:

• Praise students' attempts, especially at the beginning. Point out strengths in their written work *before* helping them find areas that need improvement. Assure students that their writing will improve, and that writing is a skill that takes time and practice to learn.

• Guide students to see that *writing is a process that begins with thinking*, and help them learn organizational strategies that allow them to collect their thoughts before they write.

- Often, a composition that is weak in many ways nonetheless contains one element that is particularly praiseworthy: a descriptive phrase that is especially colorful; a unique word choice; a powerful or moving sentence about an event. Look for these "unexpected gems" and share them with the class. Reading these passages aloud will demonstrate some elements of good writing and boost the confidence of less fluent writers. Try to read from every student's work at least once. Telling students that any student work that is read aloud will be read anonymously will help them feel comfortable with this practice.

- Start slowly, and build over time. Adapt the sequence and complexity of writing activities to match your students' abilities. Move from sentence to paragraph to composition slowly, recognizing that different students will progress at different paces. When students do show increased fluency and confidence, though, be sure to offer them writing assignments that challenge them appropriately, while providing the support they will need to succeed on these. (See "Adapting Lessons to Meet Students' Individual Needs" in this teacher's guide for a discussion of scaffolding.)

EVALUATION AND ASSESSMENT

Establishing a Baseline. At the beginning of the school year you may wish to establish the baseline proficiency of the students in your class. This will help you assess individual students' strengths and weaknesses, and may help you employ grouping strategies that will help your students grow as writers. To establish a baseline, give all students the same writing prompt to respond to. The prompt should not require any specialized knowledge or vocabulary. (Example: *What is your earliest memory? Write about it.*) Responses will give you an indication of each student's writing fluency. Compare this initial assignment with subsequent writing efforts to help you assess progress.

Using a Rubric and Checklists to Evaluate Writing. A rubric that can be used to help you evaluate the overall quality of students' compositions has been provided on page 61 of this teacher's guide. Evaluation checklists, which have been provided for each writing lesson in the student book, begin on page 62 of this teacher's guide. It is recommended that you duplicate a set of these checklists for each student at the beginning of the year; they will serve as both evaluation and record-keeping forms.

Student Self-Evaluation. Periodically, have students compare their early work with their later writing so that they, too, can be aware of their growth as writers. You may choose occasionally to have more fluent writers use the checklists to evaluate their own work. Alternately, have more advanced students construct their own criteria by asking them questions such as: *What makes an outstanding personal narrative?* Encourage students to use their criteria as guides when evaluating their own work and the work of their peers.

REMEDIATION AND PRACTICE

Grammar and Mechanics. Most developing writers need ongoing practice with basic grammar and mechanics skills, such as avoiding run-ons and sentence fragments, using high-utility homophones such as *it's* and *its* properly, and using commas correctly. As you identify specific skills that need improvement, assign one or more of the following remediation activities:

- Have students review the appropriate section(s) of the Handbook and study the practice exercises. Give them five additional practice items to complete for each skill.

- Have students complete a lesson that focuses on the targeted skill a second time. Repeat this until students can answer each item correctly.

- Help students create a list of their own "trouble spots," including references to the Handbook Guides, and use the list whenever they revise their writing. As they achieve mastery with specific skills, they can remove those "trouble spots" from the list.

Content. Developing writers often struggle with organizing and sequencing the flow of their ideas. Help them to see writing as a thinking process. Visual mapping activities such as word webs, outlines, and Venn diagrams can help students organize their thoughts and understand the vital connection between thinking and writing. If possible, evaluate completed writing with students individually. Help them identify ideas that are repeated, contradictory, out of sequence, or off the topic. Then have students rewrite the piece, based on their own observations.

Practice. Following are some suggestions for helping students practice their writing and revising skills outside the lessons:

- Provide additional writing prompts to reinforce demand writing skills. Encourage students to make a habit of using the *Plan* and *Write* steps to help them organize their thoughts quickly before they begin writing.

- Have students rewrite exercise sentences from an instructional lesson as paragraphs, adding transition words, an introduction, and a conclusion. Encourage them to consider resequencing the sentences to improve the flow of ideas.

- To provide proofreading practice, pair students and have each one rewrite a paragraph from a book, omitting all punctuation and capitalization and inserting some spelling errors. Partners can trade passages, correct them, and then check their work against the original passage.

Adapting Lessons to Meet Students' Individual Needs

Students learn best when lessons encourage them to stretch for new knowledge *that is within their reach if they stretch.* This process of having to work to grasp a concept ensures engagement, develops thinking processes, and prepares the student for the next stretch he or she will need to make.

Education researchers, such as Dr. Robert Rueda of the University of Southern California, have explained the process of supporting students' learning as being similar to constructing **scaffolding.** The best kind of help puts each student within reach—but not always easy reach—of important concepts and information.

What makes this process challenging for a teacher are the many differences among students in any class. Students bring with them widely differing literacy skills and background knowledge; they learn in different ways, and they learn at different paces. Adjusting each lesson to provide just the right amount of challenge to each student is a goal unlikely to be met in a real-world classroom.

Nevertheless, you can make instruction significantly more effective by keeping in mind the effectiveness

of scaffolding and becoming aware of students' preferred modes of learning and varying levels of proficiency.

ADDRESSING THE THREE MODALITIES

Over the years many teachers have found it helpful to tailor some activities to students who learn best *visually,* some to students who learn best *aurally,* and some to students who learn best *kinesthetically.* Lessons in *Practical Guide to Better English* can be adapted in a number of ways to address each of these modalities. Here are a few suggestions:

Visual. As a part of each lesson on sentence structure, show students how to diagram a simple sentence with that structure. Diagramming was formerly thought of by some as tedious and esoteric; and it can be, with complex sentences. But a sentence diagram is actually a graphic organizer—a highly visual way of illustrating how basic sentence elements relate to one another. Showing students how to diagram simple sentences is likely to be of great help to those who are visual learners.

Aural. In lessons on parts of speech and on related word forms, read aloud lesson sentences using nonsense substitutions to highlight functions and inflected endings.

The *bink binked* a *bink.*

The *bink binked binkly.*

The *binky bink* was *binked* by a *bink.*

Students can be asked to replace the nonsense forms with real words, and explain how they decided what kind of word to use.

Kinesthetic. To help students understand how different parts of speech and kinds of phrases function in sentences, have students cut sentences from the lesson apart into words and phrases, and then see how many sentences *different from the originals* they can put together using clear tape.

ADAPTING LESSONS FOR STUDENTS WITH LESS PROFICIENCY

Users of this program are likely to have already developed a number of effective ways to help less advanced students gain benefit from lessons they are unable to complete independently. Following are some suggestions that may or may not be new to you.

- Read Handbook sections, lesson directions, and any examples aloud. Have a volunteer write the first lesson item on the board and model completing it. Then have students work in pairs to complete the lesson items.

- Have students work in a small group led by a peer tutor. Group members can take turns completing items, showing their responses to the group, and explaining their answer choices.

- Using the chalkboard, model completing the first five items of a lesson. Have students watch with their books closed. Then have them open their books and work on those same five items, plus the next five. Have them then stop, check, and discuss their work. Finally, have them complete the remaining items.

- For the first item, write a correct response and an incorrect response on the chalkboard. Have students raise their hands when you point to the response they believe is correct. Ask a student who identified the correct response to tell why it is correct. Continue this process until students seem confident they can complete the remaining items independently.

Helping Students Who Are Acquiring English

Older students who are acquiring English face a special challenge. The content load of the texts for which they are responsible in classes or on the job is typically heavy, but their oral and written English skills may be at a relatively low level. Yet they have a compelling need to understand and make use of the information in such texts because long-term success in the workplace depends on their being able to do so.

For these students to have the best possible chance of succeeding in a course of study, both the materials and the instruction must be considerate of their needs and abilities. Simplicity and clarity are extremely important. As Robert Rueda, professor of educational psychology at the University of Southern California has written, "Trying to learn difficult academic content at the same time one is trying to understand an unfamiliar language tends to overload the capacity to learn."

The lessons and Handbook Guides in the *Practical Guide to Better English* program have been written and structured to meet the needs of second language learners and their teachers. Every effort has been made to simplify language and structure and eliminate obstacles to understanding. Nevertheless, because the program deals with a complex subject—the structure and rules of the English language—students acquiring English are likely to experience some language-related difficulties in the course of completing lessons. Your ability to recognize that a student is having difficulty and offer appropriate help is one of the most important elements in the instructional process. The teaching procedures listed below have been shown to be of significant value to second language learners, both in helping them complete coursework successfully and in advancing their acquisition of English.

ORAL LANGUAGE DEVELOPMENT

- Read aloud examples and answers.

- Ask students to answer items orally.

- Model effective oral reading and pronunciation by reading passages aloud.

- Use repetition—have students repeat what they hear.

- For those students with lesser levels of English proficiency, have them respond orally to questions whose answers they have already learned.

VOCABULARY DEVELOPMENT

- Identify and review key vocabulary and concepts for exercises; write these words on the chalkboard; use pictures or props to illustrate word meanings when possible.

- Discuss the meanings of unfamiliar expressions and idioms.

- Discuss troublesome words: multiple meaning words, homophones, and homographs. Guide students to use context to determine meaning.

- Direct students to develop webs of related words for use in writing activities.

- Encourage students to keep lists of words they want to make part of their active vocabulary; encourage them to use these in class discussions and writing activities.

CONCEPT DEVELOPMENT AND SKILL INSTRUCTION (SCAFFOLDING)

- Activate students' prior knowledge of familiar subjects through class discussion.

- Discuss with students topics likely to be unfamiliar to them before directing them to read or write about those topics.

- Read aloud and model activities with volunteers.

- Redefine terms orally.

- Speak clearly and pause often.

- Say the same thing in different ways.

- Ask yes/no questions to engage students.

- Use visual learning cues—drawings, photographs, illustrations—when possible.

- Dramatize meaning through facial expressions, pantomime, and gestures.

- Check comprehension frequently by asking questions.

- Remind students of particular things to do or avoid doing.

- Have students dictate their ideas for writing activities before they begin the task of writing.

- Encourage students to make comparisons between their primary language and English.

COOPERATIVE LEARNING

- Have students work with English-proficient partners on proofreading activities.

- Offer opportunities for students who share the same primary language to work on skill lessons and activities together.

AWARENESS OF CULTURAL DIFFERENCES

- Be prepared for different personal responses to exercise items.

- Keep in mind that students' difficulties in responding to a lesson topic may be the result of cultural differences rather than lack of comprehension of vocabulary.

Assessment

A cornerstone of the *Practical Guide to Better English* program is ongoing assessment that provides a clear picture of each student's level of proficiency with specific English language skills and writing tasks. The program's formal assessment instruments enable you to adjust instruction in each unit to fit students' needs as well as monitor their progress. Informal assessment, which can take many forms, including those outlined on the next page, provides additional information about students' strengths and weaknesses. Assessment of the writing activities enables both teachers and students to recognize growth in language proficiency as well as identify areas in which more work is needed.

FORMAL ASSESSMENT IN *PRACTICAL GUIDE TO BETTER ENGLISH*

Diagnostic Tests. Each unit's diagnostic test provides a quick snapshot of students' familiarity with the skills covered in that unit. Reproducible masters of diagnostic tests for Units I–VIII appear on pages 24–53 in this teacher's guide. To administer the diagnostic text for a unit, give each student a copy of the test; have students complete all sections independently; then collect the tests and check students' answers. Answers to these tests appear on pages 56–57 of this teacher's guide. Afterward, look at each student's errors. On the basis of the patterns you note, you may want to adjust instruction in one of these ways:

- If a small group of students show by their responses that they are not at all familiar with a skill, you may want to provide a pre-lesson tutorial on that skill for those students.

- If the majority of the class indicate through their responses that they are not at all familiar with a skill that will be taught in the unit, you may want to utilize one of the whole-class guided learning procedures outlined in "Adapting Lessons to Meet Students' Individual Needs" when presenting that lesson.

- If some students show by their responses that they are already familiar with a skill to be taught, you may want to have them either skip that lesson, complete it as homework, or serve as peer tutors for that lesson to students who need work on that skill.

Be sure to retain students' tests so you can compare their performance on each section with their performance on the same section of the achievement test, which is to be administered at the conclusion of the unit. Use the record-keeping form on page 60 of this teacher's guide to record test scores.

Achievement Tests. Each unit's achievement test checks students' progress with the unit skills and provides information that can be used to develop a plan for targeted remediation and additional practice. Reproducible masters of achievement tests for Units I–VIII appear on pages 26–55 in this teacher's guide. Administer the achievement test for a unit in the same manner as the diagnostic test. Answers for these tests appear on pages 58–59. Afterward, compare each student's performance on each section with his or her performance on the same section of the diagnostic test. Note areas of progress and areas in which remedial work is needed. For students needing remediation in a particular skill, it is recommended that you repeat the lesson that focuses on the problem area, and have them work through the exercises a second time using one of the procedures outlined in the section headed "Adapting Lessons for Students with Less Proficiency" in this teacher's guide.

You may want to record each student's performance on the individual student record-keeping form on page 60 of this teacher's guide.

Writing Assessment. Suggestions for assessing students' writing progress appear in the section entitled "Teaching Composition" on pages 17–20 of this teacher's guide. A rubric and checklists for evaluating writing lessons appear on pages 61–65.

INFORMAL ASSESSMENT IN *PRACTICAL GUIDE TO BETTER ENGLISH*

Observation/Holistic Assessment. Observing and making note of individual students' performance on various tasks during the course of each unit is an important part of the assessment process.

Among the many productive focuses for informal observation are the following:

- Students' performance on the exercises, including how much help they need to be able to complete the exercises.

- Students' knowledge of grammar, usage, and mechanics concepts as evidenced in their responses to questions asked of them.

- Students' willingness to try using new vocabulary and specialized terms in oral discussions.

- Students' use of correct and incorrect word forms in class discussions.

- Students' use of correct and incorrect word forms in written work for literature study, and in papers written for other classes.

- Students' attitude toward completing the exercises and writing tasks.

- Students' choice of books and magazines for independent reading.

Space for recording observations and anecdotal records of progress is provided on the individual student record-keeping form.

Student Self-Monitoring. Students can monitor themselves as they work through the unit by making note of what they do and do not understand, either in a personal journal or directly on the lesson pages. Encourage them also to use the practice items in the Handbook Guides as a quick method of assessing whether they understand a new rule or concept. The score chart that appears on page 176 of the student book provides a further means for students to keep track of personal progress.

UNIT 1
Diagnostic Test, page 1

PART I Write *yes* before each group of words that is a sentence. Write *no* before each group of words that is not a sentence.

_____ 1. The ground shook violently during the earthquake.

_____ 2. Trees wobbling and windows shattering.

_____ 3. The movement caused damage to several buildings.

_____ 4. Cracks in windows and walls.

PART II Draw one line under each common noun and two lines under each proper noun.

5. California is known for its earthquakes.

6. The San Andreas Fault is the longest fault in the state.

7 In April of 1906, a huge tremor shook San Francisco, starting many fires.

8. Was it the most destructive quake in the history of the United States?

PART III Draw one line under the complete subject in each sentence. Draw a second line under the simple subject.

9. People can prepare for natural disasters in many ways.

10. Some families equip their homes with emergency supplies.

11. Family members plan escape routes.

PART IV Underline the complete predicate in each sentence below. On the line after the sentence, write the simple predicate.

12. Students and teachers conduct drills of emergency procedures. _____

13. Some neighborhoods have organized special disaster response plans. _____

14. Certain buildings may be used as gathering places after a disaster. _____

PRACTICAL GUIDE TO BETTER ENGLISH

PART V In each sentence below, draw one line under the complete subject and two lines under the complete predicate.

15.   Earthquakes strike without warning.

16.   A series of small quakes may precede a large quake.

17.   Preparation can save property and lives.

PART VI Place the appropriate end mark at the end of each sentence. On the line write *declarative, interrogative, imperative,* or *exclamatory* to show what kind of sentence it is.

18.   Did you feel that tremor___   _____

19.   That was just a small earthquake___   _____

20.   How frightening it was___   _____

21.   Watch for falling objects___   _____

PART VII Add commas to set off names in direct address, *yes* or *no*, words or phrases in a series, and appositives.

22.   "Grace did you see the lightning last night?" asked Zack.

23.   "Yes I was walking outside with Scruffy and Spot my dogs," said Grace.

24.   "They barked jumped and growled," she said.

PART VIII If the italicized word is singular, write the plural form on the line. If the italicized word is plural, write the singular form on the line.

25.   The *pony* moved uneasily in its stall. _____

26.   The sow squealed as if her *life* was in danger. _____

27.   The *sheep* bleated and jumped at the gate of their pen. _____

PART IX Draw a line under each word that should begin with a capital letter

28.   the tornado touched down in kansas on a warm wednesday in june.

29.   brad west and his sisters, olivia and heidi, were at luke's hamburger haven.

30.   the morelands' cattle farm on pozer road was miraculously left untouched.

UNIT I
Achievement Test, page 1

PART I   Write *yes* before each group of words that is a sentence. Write *no* before each group of words that is not a sentence.

_____   1.   Abraham Lincoln was one of America's greatest presidents.

_____   2.   A woodcutter as a young man, a lawyer by profession.

_____   3.   Born in a small log cabin in 1809.

_____   4.   Lincoln was President during the Civil War.

PART II   Draw one line under each common noun and two lines under each proper noun.

5.   Abraham Lincoln was born in a cabin in Kentucky.

6.   He was born in the month of February.

7   President's Day honors Abraham Lincoln and George Washington.

8.   This holiday is celebrated with ceremonies throughout the United States.

PART III   Draw one line under the complete subject in each sentence. Draw a second line under the simple subject.

9.   Lincoln's family moved to Indiana in 1816.

10.   Life was rough and dangerous on the Indiana frontier.

11.   Wild animals posed a constant threat.

PART IV   Underline the complete predicate in each sentence below. On the line after the sentence, write the simple predicate.

12.   Several fine writers have written biographies of Lincoln. _____

13.   Lincoln had less than a year of formal education. _____

14.   He taught himself reading and writing. _____

PRACTICAL GUIDE TO BETTER ENGLISH

PART V In each sentence below, draw one line under the complete subject and two lines under the complete predicate.

15. Young Abe Lincoln had a keen mind.

16. He became a lawyer in 1836.

17. This son of the frontier entered politics several years later.

PART VI Place the appropriate end mark at the end of each sentence. On the line write *declarative*, *interrogative*, *imperative*, or *exclamatory* to show what kind of sentence it is.

18. Lincoln was personally opposed to slavery__   _____

19. How hard he argued against it__   _____

20. When did Lincoln become President__   _____

21. Find that date in the encyclopedia__   _____

PART VII Add commas to set off names in direct address, *yes* or *no*, words or phrases in a series, and appositives.

22. "Do you admire Abraham Lincoln Alison?" asked Duke.

23. "Yes he guided the nation during the Civil War its darkest hour," Alison replied.

24. "He led with wisdom intelligence and strength," she continued.

PART VIII If the italicized word is singular, write the plural form on the line. If the italicized word is plural, write the singular form on the line.

25. The Civil War caused great loss of *life.* _____

26. Because of the war, a friend could become an *enemy.* _____

27. A *child* could lose a father or a mother. _____

PART IX Draw a line under each word that should begin with a capital letter

28. robert E. Lee surrendered to ulysses S. grant on april 9, 1865.

29. the surrender took place in appomattox, virginia.

30. president lincoln was assassinated in washington, D.C., on april 14, 1865.

PRACTICAL GUIDE TO BETTER ENGLISH

UNIT II
Diagnostic Test, page 1

PART I   Draw one line under the complete subject and two lines under the complete predicate in each sentence. After the sentence, write the simple subject and the simple predicate.

simple subject   *simple predicate*

1.   The Wolverines will face the Vikings in the playoff game.   _____   _____

2.   The band members have been practicing all week.   _____   _____

3.   The school band is gathering on the field.   _____   _____

PART II   Draw a line under the simple predicate in each sentence. On the line, write each helping verb.

4.   The tuba players are wearing Viking helmets.   _____

5.   The drummers have been disguised as wolverines.   _____

6.   The drummers will chase the tuba players around the field.   _____

PART III   Draw a line under the appropriate verb in parentheses.

7.   The tuba (is, are) a large, awkward instrument.

8.   The drummers (is, are) skilled and energetic.

9.   The members of the band (is, are) tired now.

PART IV   Draw a line under the appropriate verb in parentheses.

10.   The band's performance (was, were) exceptional.

11.   Onlookers (was, were) entertained by their antics.

12.   Even the Vikings (was, were) amused.

PART V   Write the possessive form of the word at the left, and add a word to show something possessed or owned.

13.   airplane   _____

14.   lawyers   _____

15.   women   _____

PRACTICAL GUIDE TO BETTER ENGLISH

PART VI Write the contractions of the following words.

16.   we are   _____

17.   have not   _____

18.   does not   _____

PART VII Draw a line under the appropriate pronoun in parentheses.

19.   Stuart and (I, me) were in the middle school orchestra together.

20.   (He, Him) and his sisters learned to play the piano at an early age.

21.   Was it (he, him) who performed in the talent show?

PART VIII In each sentence below, underline each simple subject once and each simple predicate twice. The sentence may contain a compound subject, a compound predicate, or both.

22.   David and Jamie studied music and played together for many years.

23.   A parade or a picnic can be an enjoyable event for musicians.

24.   A band with horn players adds spirit and encourages clapping.

PART IX Draw a line under the simple subject in each sentence. On the line, write the simple predicate.

25.   Can you identify all the instruments in the orchestra?   _____

26.   There are violas and cellos in the string section.   _____

27.   They can produce beautiful low tones.   _____

PART X Underline the appropriate form of the word in parentheses.

28.   David (took, taken) guitar lessons for five years.

29.   He has (become, became) an accomplished musician.

30.   Music has (gave, given) him a creative outlet.

PRACTICAL GUIDE TO BETTER ENGLISH

UNIT II
Achievement Test, page 1

PART I Draw one line under the complete subject and two lines under the complete predicate in each sentence. After the sentence, write the simple subject and the simple predicate.

simple subject   *simple predicate*

1. Many wild creatures are found in cities.   _____ _____

2. Raccoons live quite comfortably in urban parks.   _____ _____

3. Opossums have been seen in city neighborhoods, too.   _____ _____

PART II Draw a line under the simple predicate in each sentence. On the line, write each helping verb.

4. Migrating birds have stopped at that pond.   _____

5. I have been watching a pair of wood ducks.   _____

6. They will continue their journey soon.   _____

PART III Draw a line under the appropriate verb in parentheses.

7. Fall and spring (is, are) good times for birdwatching.

8. Geese (is, are) migrating birds.

9. That bird above the trees (is, are) a Canada goose.

PART IV Draw a line under the appropriate verb in parentheses.

10. We (was, were) awakened last night by a great commotion.

11. A raccoon (was, were) raiding someone's trash can.

12. The neighbor's dogs (was, were) barking wildly.

PART V Write the possessive form of the word at the left, and add a word to show something possessed or owned.

13. men   _____

14. raccoons   _____

15. officer   _____

PRACTICAL GUIDE TO BETTER ENGLISH

Unit II Achievement Test, page 2

PART VI Write the contractions of the following words.

16. you will _____

17. I am _____

18. cannot _____

PART VII Draw a line under the appropriate pronoun in parentheses.

19. My neighbors and (I, me) were once plagued by raccoons.

20. Did (they, them) eat the cats' food?

21. It was (me, I) who found a solution.

PART VIII In each sentence below, underline each simple subject once and each simple predicate twice. The sentence may contain a compound subject, a compound predicate, or both.

22. Raccoons and opossums are nocturnal.

23. They prowl at night and search for food in the areas near their homes.

24. My neighbors and I cover our trash cans and close the pet doors.

PART IX Draw a line under the simple subject in each sentence. On the line, write the simple predicate.

25. There are many ugly holes in my lawn. _____

26. They are the work of raccoons. _____

27. Do the raccoons dig for roots and insects? _____

PART X Underline the appropriate form of the word in parentheses.

28. Last year I (begun, began) an urban wildlife journal.

29. It has (grown, grew) to three volumes.

30. I have (did, done) sketches of dozens of wild creatures.

PRACTICAL GUIDE TO BETTER ENGLISH

UNIT III
Diagnostic Test, page 1

PART I Draw one line under each verb or verb phrase. Draw two lines under each direct object.

1. Coach Glen had told the team about the upcoming cross-country race.

2. Ari, the team captain, visited Coach Glen in her office.

3. She told Ari about the training schedule.

4. Ari led the team through several conditioning drills.

PART II Draw one line under each verb or verb phrase. Underline each direct object twice.

5. Coach Glen called me into her office.

6. Ari will drive us to the game.

7. Brett led them in a series of exercises.

PART III On the lines, write the simple subject, the simple predicate, and the direct object of each sentence, in that order.

8. We practiced soccer for many hours.

   _____   _____   _____

9. Our team won our first two games without a struggle.

   _____   _____   _____

10. Our goalie hurt her ankle in the third game.

   _____   _____   _____

11. The other team quickly scored two goals.

   _____   _____   _____

PART IV Draw a line under the prepositional phrase in each sentence. Draw a second line under the object of the preposition.

12. Ari kicked the ball toward the goal.

13. The goalie made a futile dive for the ball.

14. The crowd in the far stands cheered enthusiastically.

PRACTICAL GUIDE TO BETTER ENGLISH

PART V   Draw a line under the pronoun that correctly completes each sentence.

15.   Melissa and (I, me) like to play water polo.

16.   Roger met (she, her) and (me, I) at four o'clock.

17.   Roger called (they, them) for directions.

18.   Water polo is a good game for (us, we).

PART VI   Think about the underlined pronoun in each sentence. Then draw a line under the word or phrase in parentheses that tells what kind of pronoun it is.

19.   Roy taught <u>himself</u> to play chess.   (compound personal, interrogative)

20.   <u>Which</u> chess piece is most useful?   (interrogative, compound personal)

21.   <u>This</u> is the queen, the most powerful piece on the board.   (demonstrative, interrogative)

22.   <u>Who</u> is the best chess player in the world?   (demonstrative, interrogative)

PART VII   Rewrite the sentences, replacing nouns with pronouns so that the sentences sound better.

23.   Roy brought Roy's chessboard to the park.

        _____

24.   Roy challenged Anna to a match, and Anna accepted.

        _____

25.   First Anna defeated Roy, and then Roy defeated Anna.

        _____

        _____

PART VIII   Punctuate the following sentences and draw a line under each word that should begin with a capital letter.

26.   every july there is a pogo stick exhibition in winslow park

27.   wasn't ms tanaka planning to hop across the united states

28.   yes she had begun her journey in sarasota florida

PART IX   Add quotation marks and other punctuation as needed. Draw a line under each word that should begin with a capital letter.

29.   my favorite hobby is mountain biking Mari said to Lois

30.   Lois told Mari that she had never ridden a mountain bike

PRACTICAL GUIDE TO BETTER ENGLISH

UNIT III
Achievement Test, page 1

PART I Draw one line under each verb or verb phrase. Draw two lines under each direct object.

1. Captain Drotning bought a book about figure drawing.

2. She practiced drawing after work every day.

3. She noticed real improvement in her work after three weeks.

4. Myra, Captain Drotning's cousin, is studying design at night.

PART II Draw one line under each verb or verb phrase. Underline each direct object twice.

5. Rachel called me on the telephone.

6. She will meet you at the book store.

7. My art teacher invited us to her opening.

PART III On the lines, write the simple subject, the simple predicate, and the direct object of each sentence, in that order.

8. We will buy a book of Leonardo da Vinci's work.

    _____ _____ _____

9. Leonardo created many famous paintings.

    _____ _____ _____

10. He also designed innovative machines.

    _____ _____ _____

11. He even sketched an idea for a flying machine.

    _____ _____ _____

PART IV Draw a line under the prepositional phrase in each sentence. Draw a second line under the object of the preposition.

12. This drawing of a human shoulder is quite accurate.

13. Leonardo studied anatomy in great detail.

14. That drawing shows his idea for a moveable bridge.

PRACTICAL GUIDE TO BETTER ENGLISH

PART V   Draw a line under the pronoun that correctly completes each sentence.

15.   Rachel and (I, me) were impressed by the book.

16.   Our teacher told (we, us) about the locations of the original drawings.

17.   We can only view (they, them) in books.

18.   Will anyone offer a free trip to Italy to (she, her) and (me, I)?

PART VI   Think about the underlined pronoun in each sentence. Then draw a line under the word or phrase in parentheses that tells what kind of pronoun it is.

19.   Rachel taught <u>herself</u> to draw.   (compound personal, interrogative)

20.   <u>Which</u> drawing is your favorite?   (interrogative, compound personal)

21.   <u>This</u> is the best drawing.   (demonstrative, interrogative)

22.   <u>Who</u> is the most famous artist of all time?   (demonstrative, interrogative)

PART VII   Rewrite the sentences, replacing nouns with pronouns so that the sentences sound better.

23.   Gerald brought Gerald's paint set to school.

_____

24.   Susan asked Gerald to help Susan on a project.

_____

25.   Susan mixed paints for Gerald, and then Gerald mixed paints for Susan.

_____

_____

PART VIII   Punctuate the following sentences and draw a line under each word that should begin with a capital letter.

26.   leonardo was born near florence italy

27.   didnt leonardo live in tours france later in his life

28.   yes he lived there and he also lived in milan italy

PART IX   Add quotation marks and other punctuation as needed. Draw a line under each word that should begin with a capital letter.

29.   my favorite artist is Michelangelo I said to Rachel

30.   she told me that she admires his work, too

PRACTICAL GUIDE TO BETTER ENGLISH

UNIT IV
Diagnostic Test, page 1

PART I In each sentence, draw one line under the simple subject and two lines under the simple predicate. Circle any direct object.

1. Some trains can carry passengers at very high speeds.

2. Overhead wires supply the electricity for these trains.

3. I bought a ticket to Chicago.

PART II Draw a line under the properly spelled word in each pair. Use a dictionary; do not guess.

4. valuable   valuble

5. lissen   listen

6. absense   absence

PART III Divide each of the following words into syllables. Use a dictionary to help you. Put an X on the line after a word that should not be divided.

7. selfish   _____

8. child   _____

9. passed   _____

10. ladder   _____

PART IV Write the respelling of each word as given in your dictionary. Add any diacritical marks and accent marks. If two pronunciations are given, list both.

11. drain   _____

12. block   _____

13. consist   _____

PART V Draw a line under the adjectives in the sentences below. Do not underline articles. On the line below each adjective, write the noun it modifies. More than one adjective may modify the same noun.

14. I heard the shrill whistle of the sleek train.

_____

15. The crowded station was packed with weary uncomfortable commuters.

_____

16. A small child waved enthusiastically to the elderly engineer.

_____

PRACTICAL GUIDE TO BETTER ENGLISH

PART VI Draw a line under each possessive noun. Draw two lines under each possessive pronoun. On the line below each one, write the noun it modifies.

17. Pablo's shiny bicycle stood near the starting line.

   _____

18. Pablo put on his helmet.

   _____

19. He listened eagerly to the instructor's thoughtful advice.

   _____

PART VII Read the paragraph below. Underline each adjective. Do not underline articles.

20-22. A hard, steady rain fell today. Now the streets glisten in the cool darkness. The tires of cars make a soft whirr on the wet streets.

PART VIII Draw a line under the appropriate form of *lie* or *lay* in parentheses.

23. Yesterday Gabriel (lay, laid) on a cloth underneath the car.

24. He carefully (lay, laid) his tools next to him on the ground.

25. Then he saw an extra bolt (laying, lying) next to the toolbox.

PART IX Draw a line under the appropriate pronoun in parentheses.

26. Susanna and (I, me) ride the bus to work.

27. Our friend Nick showed (we, us) a faster route on the L line.

28. A shorter bus ride makes (us, we) commuters happy.

PART X Draw a line under the appropriate form of the verbs in parentheses.

29. My sister (flew, flown) her new box kite at the park on Saturday.

30. I have not (saw, seen) that kite yet.

PRACTICAL GUIDE TO BETTER ENGLISH

UNIT IV
Achievement Test, *page 1*

PART I In each sentence, draw one line under the simple subject and two lines under the simple predicate. Circle any direct object.

1. Ricardo's uncle found some old pottery at a construction site.

2. His discovery excited local historians.

3. Ricardo is studying ancient civilizations in school.

PART II Draw a line under the properly spelled word in each pair. Use a dictionary; do not guess.

4. evry   every

5. courius   curious

6. chief   cheif

PART III Divide each of the following words into syllables. Use a dictionary to help you. Put an X on the line after a word that should not be divided.

7. welcome   _____

8. style   _____

9. missed   _____

10. logger   _____

PART IV Write the respelling of each word as given in your dictionary. Add any diacritical marks and accent marks. If two pronunciations are given, list both.

11. display   _____

12. onion   _____

13. blame   _____

PART V Draw a line under the adjectives in the sentences below. Do not underline articles. On the line below each adjective, write the noun it modifies. More than one adjective may modify the same noun.

14. I found small shards from a blue bowl.

_____

15. Paula found three shiny arrowheads in a deep ditch.

_____

16. We gave the interesting artifacts to the local museum.

_____

PRACTICAL GUIDE TO BETTER ENGLISH

PART VI Draw a line under each possessive noun. Draw two lines under each possessive pronoun. On the line below each one, write the noun it modifies.

17. Ricardo's classes at the university are challenging.

_____

18. His professors require a lot of work.

_____

19. This week's writing assignments will cause students to spend their evenings in the library.

_____

PART VII Read the paragraph below. Underline each adjective. Do not underline articles.

20-22. Construction has stopped on the new mall. Eager historians are now exploring the site for objects from the distant past. The hole dug by huge machines has already yielded several treasures.

PART VIII Draw a line under the appropriate form of *lie* or *lay* in parentheses.

23. Please (lie, lay) that arrowhead on the cloth.

24. I found it (lying, laying) in a pile of rocks.

25. It has probably (laid, lain) there for centuries.

PART IX Draw a line under the appropriate pronoun in parentheses.

26. Ricardo (hisself, himself) found that tin cup.

27. (We, Us) historians were surprised by the find.

28. Its presence in the pit gave (we, us) new information.

PART X Draw a line under the appropriate form of the verbs in parentheses.

29. An artist has (drew, drawn) pictures of some artifacts.

30. It (taken, took) us two weeks to complete our exploration.

PRACTICAL GUIDE TO BETTER ENGLISH

UNIT V
Diagnostic Test, page 1

PART I   Write the contraction for each pair of words. Then complete each sentence by underlining the contraction that fits there.

1.   they are   _____

2.   you will   _____

3.   she would   _____

4.   who is   _____

5.   Can you tell me (who's, whose) hat this is?

6.   (Its, It's) Carmelo's hat.

PART II   Underline each adverb in the following sentences. Below each adverb, write the verb or verb phrase it modifies.

7.   Carmelo pruned the plum trees skillfully.

     _____

8.   He sometimes works in the pear orchards.

     _____

9.   He will prune the peach tree tomorrow.

     _____

PART III   In each sentence, an adverb that modifies an adjective or another adverb has been underlined. On the first line after the sentence, write the word it modifies. On the second line, write *adjective* or *adverb* to show what kind of word it is.

10.   Ben is a <u>very</u> capable chef.   _____ _____

11.   His desserts are <u>quite</u> delicious.   _____ _____

12.   Are you surprised that he cooks <u>so</u> expertly?   _____ _____

PART IV   Draw a line under the adverb in each sentence. On the first line after the sentence, write the word it modifies. On the second line, write *verb* or *adjective* to tell what part of speech has been modified.

13.   Tanya mowed the lawn yesterday.   _____ _____

14.   Sam worked nearby in the flower garden.   _____ _____

15.   Sam's roses are extremely beautiful.   _____ _____

PRACTICAL GUIDE TO BETTER ENGLISH

PART V Fill each blank with the appropriate word in parentheses.

16. (great, greatly) The _____ architect _____ overestimated his assistants' abilities.

17. (clear, clearly) They _____ had no _____ idea of how to solve the problem.

18. (good, well) They tried to offer a _____ solution, but they didn't perform very _____.

PART VI Punctuate the following sentences and underline each word that should begin with a capital letter.

19. margaret do you make deliveries to many north american cities asked tomás

20. yes we've shipped our products to miami florida and montreal quebec replied margaret

21. we've also made deliveries in vancouver british columbia and san diego california she said

PART VII Draw a line through the unnecessary word in each sentence.

22. These here petunias are beautiful.

23. Spring is like my favorite season.

24. My aunt she is an expert gardener.

PART VIII Underline the appropriate word in parentheses.

25. (Pat and me, Pat and I) are in training together.

26. (Its, It's) challenging work.

27. (Your, You're) going to need those gloves.

PART IX Draw a line under each appropriate word in parentheses.

28. (May, Can) I see the manual?

29. Who (taught, learned) you to roll up the hoses?

30. My friend Walter (bought, buyed) a sprayer last week.

PRACTICAL GUIDE TO BETTER ENGLISH

UNIT V
Achievement Test, *page 1*

PART I Write the contraction for each pair of words. Then complete each sentence by underlining the contraction that fits there.

1. he had   _____

2. you are   _____

3. what is   _____

4. there is   _____

5. (Your, You're) going to like this movie.

6. (Its, It's) about an Arctic adventure.

PART II Underline each adverb in the following sentences. Below each adverb, write the verb or verb phrase it modifies.

7. The temperature dropped rapidly.

    _____

8. Winter storms sometimes cause power failures.

    _____

9. Soon the streams will freeze.

    _____

PART III In each sentence, an adverb that modifies an adjective or another adverb has been underlined. On the first line after the sentence, write the word it modifies. On the second line, write *adjective* or *adverb* to show what kind of word it is.

10. Captain Baumann is an <u>incredibly</u> successful explorer _____   _____

11. His accomplishments are <u>very</u> impressive.   _____   _____

12. He has escaped disaster <u>quite</u> often.   _____   _____

PART IV Draw a line under the adverb in each sentence. On the first line after the sentence, write the word it modifies. On the second line, write *verb* or *adjective* to tell what part of speech has been modified.

13. The explorers quickly constructed a snow hut.   _____   _____

14. The dogs remained outside.   _____   _____

15. Sled dogs have incredibly thick coats.   _____   _____

PRACTICAL GUIDE TO BETTER ENGLISH

PART V   Fill each blank with the appropriate word in parentheses.

16. (good, well) The explorers tried to get a _____ night's sleep, but none of them slept _____.

17. (near, nearly) The dogs _____ the hut barked _____ all night long.

18. (slight, slightly) A _____ change in plans made the men _____ nervous.

PART VI   Punctuate the following sentences and underline each word that should begin with a capital letter.

19. deanna did that story take place in sitka alaska asked rick

20. no the setting was siberia deanna replied

21. the movie was filmed in canada russia and alaska she continued

PART VII   Draw a line through the unnecessary word in each sentence.

22. That there movie was exciting.

23. My cousin he has seen it six times.

24. The story was like based on a real incident.

PART VIII   Underline the appropriate word in parentheses.

25. Is (your, you're) brother's name LaMar?

26. No, (its, it's) LaMont.

27. (LaMont and me, LaMont and I) are movie buffs.

PART IX   Draw a line under each appropriate word in parentheses.

28. LaMont has (wrote, written) a screenplay.

29. (Can, May) I read it sometime?

30. I will (learn, teach) you how to operate a video camera.

PRACTICAL GUIDE TO BETTER ENGLISH

Name_____   Date _____

UNIT VI
Diagnostic Test, page 1

PART I   Draw a line under each prepositional phrase used as an adjective. On the line, write the noun that the phrase modifies.

1.   The turtle's home is a large rock under the bridge.   _____

2.   A bench on the lake shore is a good observation spot.   _____

3.   The tree behind the bench provides shade.   _____

PART II   Draw a line under each prepositional phrase used as an adverb. On the line write the verb that the phrase modifies.

4.   Two owls made a nest inside our barn.   _____

5.   One owl flew across the yard.   _____

6.   It probably was hunting for mice.   _____

PART III   Underline the prepositional phrase in each sentence below. Place parentheses around the noun or verb it modifies. After the phrase, write *adjective* or *adverb* to show how the phrase has been used.

7.   Owls hunt prey at night.   _____

8.   They glide in silence.   _____

9.   The owls in our barn control the rodent population.   _____

PART IV   Choose the appropriate preposition and write it in the blank.

10.   (off, from) A few years ago an alligator escaped _____ a nature sanctuary.

11.   (among, between) That sanctuary was _____ Childs and Brighton.

12.   (in, into) Everyone thought the gator was hiding _____ a nearby lake.

PART V   Draw a line through each unnecessary word in the sentences.

13.   The mayor went and announced that the lake would be closed to swimmers.

14.   That there gator returned to the sanctuary on its own.

PART VI   Draw a line under the appropriate word or phrase in parentheses.

15.   I haven't (never, ever) seen such a sad-looking dog.

16.   Its previous owners (should have, should of) taken better care of it.

PART VII   Draw a line under the appropriate word in each pair of words.

17.   The dog whined (sorrowful, sorrowfully).

18.   I was (very, real) determined to find it a good home.

19.   A (nice, nicely) family answered my ad.

PART VIII   Each sentence has either a predicate noun or a predicate adjective. Draw one line under each predicate noun. Draw two lines under each predicate adjective.

20.   Dogs are wonderful pets.

21.   Retrievers are friendly.

22.   My dog is a poodle.

PART IX   Punctuate the following sentences and underline each word that should begin with a capital letter.

23.   the april edition of *national geographic* has an article about peregrine falcons said marta

24.   does it mention a group in idaho that is trying to help the falcons survive asked tyree

25.   yes and it also tells about a famous falcon in baltimore named beauregard said marta

26.   one ornithologist said that some falcons hunt near the city's new baseball park

PART X   On the lines below, rewrite the following paragraph, using appropriate forms.

27-30.

     I works at the animal shelter two day a week. Between you and I, people ain't always responsible pet owners. Many people buy exotic pets when their young and cute. When them pets get big, they abandon them. Don't never by an pet unless you understand it's needs and are prepared to care for it.

_____

_____

_____

_____

PRACTICAL GUIDE TO BETTER ENGLISH

Name_____ Date _____

UNIT VI
Achievement Test, page 1

PART I Draw a line under each prepositional phrase used as an adjective. On the line, write the noun that the phrase modifies.

1. The Air Force is one branch of the armed forces. _____

2. That plane on the ground is an F-16. _____

3. The stripes on this insignia show rank. _____

PART II Draw a line under each prepositional phrase used as an adverb. On the line write the verb that the phrase modifies.

4. My brother Derek joined the Air Force in 1992. _____

5. He trained at Lackland Air Force Base. _____

6. Those recruits will learn about military life. _____

PART III Underline the prepositional phrase in each sentence below. Place parentheses around the noun or verb it modifies. After the phrase, write *adjective* or *adverb* to show how the phrase has been used.

7. Derek studied aircraft repair for four years. _____

8. Now he lives in Hawaii. _____

9. Mechanics in the Air Force are highly skilled. _____

PART IV Choose the appropriate preposition and write it in the blank.

10. (among, between) The distance _____ Hawaii and Japan is great.

11. (of, off) One _____ my friends is a pilot.

12. (in, into) He stores his plane _____ an old barn.

PART V Draw a line through each unnecessary word in the sentences.

13. That there airplane was built in 1938.

14. My brother he told me it's a transport plane.

Unit VI Achievement Test, page 2

PART VI Draw a line under the appropriate word or phrase in parentheses.

15. I hadn't (never, ever) seen a transport plane before.

16. I should (of, have) brought my camera.

PART VII Draw a line under the appropriate word in each pair of words.

17. It was a (very, real) clear day.

18. An F-15 Eagle flew overhead with a (loudly, loud) roar.

19. "Look at that!" I cried (hoarse, hoarsely).

PART VIII Each sentence has either a predicate noun or a predicate adjective. Draw one line under each predicate noun. Draw two lines under each predicate adjective.

20. An F-15 Eagle is loud!

21. My brother is a mechanic.

22. His job seems fascinating.

PART IX Punctuate the following sentences and underline each word that should begin with a capital letter.

23. have you ever heard of jacqueline cochran derek asked

24. yes she was a famous aviation pioneer said dierdre

25. she led a team of american women pilots during world war II dierdre continued

26. derek explained that the women flew within the united states but not in europe

PART X On the lines below, rewrite the following paragraph, using appropriate forms.

27-30.

Susan work in the community garden two weekend each month. Between you and I, that job ain't easy to do. Their are always weeds to pull, and the compost it has to be turned every day if its going to become good fertilizer. I wouldn't never sign up for that there job. If you likes to spend you're time outside, it might be an good job for you.

_____

_____

_____

_____

_____

UNIT VII
Diagnostic Test, page 1

PART I Use the conjunction in parentheses to combine each pair of sentences into one sentence. You may change word order, if necessary.

1. (because) I often invite my friends for dinner. I enjoy cooking.

    _____

2. (or) Tonight I'm going to prepare paella. If I don't, I'll prepare gazpacho.

    _____

3. (until) I can't decide what to cook. I've seen what ingredients look the freshest.

    _____

PART II In each blank, write a fitting interjection from the list below.

hurry	ouch	help
hi	sorry	oh

4. "_____! The side of this pan is very hot," said Tori.

5. "_____! I forgot to warn you that the stove was on," I replied.

PART III Write the missing principal parts and present participle forms of the verbs given below.

	Present	Past	Past Participle	Present Participle
6.	*go*	_____	*gone*	_____
7.	_____	_____	*thrown*	*throwing*
8.	_____	*began*	_____	*beginning*

PART IV In each blank, write the form of the verb asked for.

9. (past of *recommend*) Shareen _____ the Indian restaurant on 16th Street.

10. (present of *make*) "The chef there _____ wonderful Indian breads," she said.

11. (past of *eat*) "The dinner I _____ there last week was delicious," she added.

12. (future of *order*) "Maybe I _____ some chicken curry," said Shareen.

PART V   Draw a line under the verb in each sentence. On the line, write the name of the perfect tense form of the verb: *present perfect, past perfect,* or *future perfect.*

13.   Sam and Irma had invited friends to breakfast.   _____

14.   None of their guests have arrived yet.   _____

15.   By midday, Sam and Irma probably will have eaten.   _____

PART VI   In each sentence, draw a line under the appropriate verb in parentheses. On the line, tell whether subject-verb agreement is singular or plural.

16.   These bagels (is, are) particularly good.   _____

17.   My friend always (brings, bring) me a bag lunch.   _____

18.   I (want, wants) a bowl of soup and a salad.   _____

PART VII   Choose the appropriate verb form and write it in the blank.

19.   (is, are) Claude and Renée _____ vegetarians.

20.   (buy, buys) They and their parents _____ mostly vegetables and grains.

21.   (does, do) Meat and fish _____ not appeal to them.

PART VIII   On the line after each word group, write whether it is a fragment, a run-on, or a comma splice.

22.   Years ago, before the invention of the microwave.   _____

23.   Microwaves save time, not everything cooks well in them.   _____

24.   Vegetables cook well in a microwave bread does not.   _____

PART IX   Draw a line under each word that should be capitalized and add necessary punctuation marks.

25.   lily has the skills of a professional chef said grant

26.   i think she should open her own restaurant in cambridge massachusetts said watty

27.   do you think she would serve pancakes waffles or omelets asked ella

PART X   Underline the verb in each sentence. On the line after the sentence, name the tense form of the verb: *past, present,* or *future.*

28.   I like Ethiopian cuisine.   _____

29.   Last month we ate at an Ethiopian restaurant.   _____

30.   I will take you there sometime.   _____

PRACTICAL GUIDE TO BETTER ENGLISH

UNIT VII
Achievement Test, page 1

PART I Use the conjunction in parentheses to combine each pair of sentences into one sentence. You may change word order, if necessary.

1. (or) We will stop at the Grand Canyon today. We will stop at Tombstone today.

    _____

2. (although) Arizona is mostly desert. Some places are heavily forested.

    _____

3. (when) We saw the Painted Desert. We visited Arizona.

    _____

PART II In each blank, write a fitting interjection from the list below.

hurry   ouch   help
hi   sorry   oh

4. "_____! That cactus is prickly!" I cried.

5. "_____! My shirt is caught on a spine!" I said.

PART III Write the missing principal parts and present participle forms of the verbs given below.

Present	Past	Past Participle	Present Participle
6. _____	*sang*	_____	*singing*
7. *fly*	_____	*flown*	_____
8. _____	_____	_____	*teaching*

PART IV In each blank, write the form of the verb asked for.

9. (past of *hike*) Yesterday we _____ into a canyon.

10. (past of *take*) I _____ photos of the desert landscape.

11. (past of *bring*) We _____ plenty of water.

12. (future of *develop*) I _____ the film at home.

PRACTICAL GUIDE TO BETTER ENGLISH

PART V   Draw a line under the verb in each sentence. On the line, write the name of the perfect tense form of the verb: *present perfect, past perfect,* or *future perfect.*

13.   We have planned our trip carefully.   _____

14.   Raul had never been to Arizona before last year.   _____

15.   By next week we will have seen most of the state.   _____

PART VI   In each sentence, draw a line under the appropriate verb in parentheses. On the line, tell whether subject-verb agreement is singular or plural.

16.   Forests (cover, covers) part of Arizona.   _____

17.   I (need, needs) more suntan lotion.   _____

18.   Those javelinas (is, are) not full-grown yet.   _____

PART VII   Choose the appropriate verb form and write it in the blank.

19.   (live, lives) The rattlesnake and the coral snake _____ in Arizona's deserts.

20.   (inhabit, inhabits) Scorpions and tarantulas _____ the warmer regions.

21.   (are, is) Raul and I _____ careful campers.

PART VIII   On the line after each word group, write whether it is a fragment, a run-on, or a comma splice.

22.   Hot, dry days and cool, clear nights.   _____

23.   I remembered my camera, I forgot the film.   _____

24.   Look at that sunset the clouds are lavender.   _____

PART IX   Draw a line under each word that should be capitalized and add necessary punctuation marks.

25.   isn't hoover dam on the colorado river asked hugh

26.   it supplies electric power to nevada arizona and california said raul

27.   tucson arizona was once a frontier fort i added

PART X   Underline the verb in each sentence. On the line after the sentence, name the tense form of the verb: *past, present,* or *future.*

28.   Arizona became a state in 1912.   _____

29.   I see rock paintings on that wall.   _____

30.   On Tuesday we will visit Tucson.   _____

UNIT VIII
Diagnostic Test, page 1

PART I Look at the words in italic type. For items 1 and 2, circle a synonym. For items 3 and 4, circle an antonym.

1. *above*   between   overhead   around   among

2. *rough*   curved   bumpy   large   right

3. *begin*   end   carry   regain   wish

4. *repair*   find   break   create   pretend

PART II Add commas to set off each quotation below. Place single quotation marks around a quotation that appears inside another quotation.

5. "Basketball" Steve said eagerly "is my favorite sport."

6. He said "When I made the team, my dad said You should be proud of yourself! "

7. "Practice" Steve continued "takes up a lot of my time."

PART III On the line after each word, write a word that has the same pronunciation but a different spelling and meaning.

8. hare _____ 10. blue _____

9. role _____ 11. stake _____

PART IV Read each sentence and think about how the italicized word is used. Then draw a line under the word in parentheses that tells what part of speech the italicized word is.

12. We *eagerly* awaited our turn on the roller coaster. (adjective, adverb)

13. The *ride* began with a slow climb up the first hill. (noun, verb)

14. At the top, our car paused *for* a few seconds. (conjunction, preposition)

15. Suddenly we *began* a terrifying plunge down the track. (verb, pronoun)

PART V In each sentence, draw one line under the simple subject and two lines under the simple predicate. If the sentence contains a direct object, write it on the line.

16. The festival attracted people from all over the city. _____

17. Floats filled the street during the parade. _____

18. Booths along the sidewalk served many kinds of food. _____

PART VI Underline the word or phrase that correctly completes each sentence.

19. The green salsa is (spicy, spicier) than the red salsa.

20. These are the (better, best) tamales I've ever had!

21. This recipe is (more complicated, most complicated) than the one I use.

PART VII Write a business letter to Ms. S. A. Nantauk, Nantauk Interactive, 444 DeLargo Street, San Francisco, California 94117. Ask her to send you a catalog of their products. Use your own name and address in the heading.

22-26. _____

_____

_____

_____

_____

_____

_____

_____

PART VIII Cross out any words that are used incorrectly in the following paragraph. Write the correct words above the incorrect ones.

27-30.

André and me wants to learn how to repair motorcycles. That there shop on Wilson Avenue offer a night course for a small fee. We signed up immediate when we heered about it. This opportunity couldnt of come at no better time.

PRACTICAL GUIDE TO BETTER ENGLISH

UNIT VIII
Achievement Test, page 1

PART I Look at the words in italic type. For items 1 and 2, circle a synonym. For items 3 and 4, circle an antonym.

1. *find*   grow   discover   drop   call

2. *scare*   inside   break   listen   frighten

3. *forgive*   replay   blame   choose   finish

4. *create*   destroy   paint   select   begin

PART II Add commas to set off each quotation below. Place single quotation marks around a quotation that appears inside another quotation.

5. "The stars" Leo said "have always fascinated me."

6. He said "When I asked my parents for a telescope, they asked Will you really use it? "

7. "That telescope" he continued "has been invaluable."

PART III On the line after each word, write a word that has the same pronunciation but a different spelling and meaning.

8. stair _____   10. scent _____

9. flower _____   11. break _____

PART IV Read each sentence and think about how the italicized word is used. Then draw a line under the word in parentheses that tells what part of speech the italicized word is.

12. *Orion* is a constellation. (noun, verb)

13. Three *bright* stars mark Orion's belt. (adjective, adverb)

14. *In* Greek mythology, Orion battled Taurus the bull. (preposition, conjunction)

15. We *see* Orion in the winter sky. (noun, verb)

PART V In each sentence, draw one line under the simple subject and two lines under the simple predicate. If the sentence contains a direct object, write it on the line.

16. Galileo studied the sky in the 1600s. _____

17. His observations of the planets confirmed
     Copernicus's conclusions. _____

18. This great scientist used a simple telescope in his studies. _____

PART VI Underline the word or phrase that correctly completes each sentence.

19. Your telescope is (better, best) than mine.

20. Sirius is (brightest, brighter) than Polaris.

21. It is the (more visible, most visible) star of all.

PART VII Write a business letter to Althea Anderson, Night Sky Productions, 1004 Aquarius Road, Columbus, Ohio 43215. Ask her to send you the free star map offered in the newspaper. Use your own name and address in the heading.

22-26. _____

_____

_____

_____

_____

_____

_____

_____

PART VIII Cross out any words that are used incorrectly in the following paragraph. Write the correct words above the incorrect ones.

27-30.

Leo and me has a telescope. We buyed it at that there flea market. It didnt cost

much, and it work real well. Were careful mapping the constellations. We couldnt of

started this project without no telescope.

PRACTICAL GUIDE TO BETTER ENGLISH

Answer Keys—Diagnostic Tests

UNIT I

1. yes   2. no   3. yes   4. no

5. <u>California</u> is known for its <u>earthquakes</u>.
6. The <u>San Andreas Fault</u> is the longest <u>fault</u> in the <u>state</u>.
7. In <u>April</u> of <u>1906</u>, a huge <u>tremor</u> shook <u>San Francisco</u>, starting many <u>fires</u>.
8. Was it the most destructive <u>quake</u> in the <u>history</u> of the <u>United States</u>?
9. <u>People</u> can prepare for natural disasters in many ways.
10. <u>Some</u> <u>families</u> equip their homes with emergency supplies.
11. <u>Family</u> <u>members</u> plan escape routes.
12. Students and teachers <u>conduct drills of emergency procedures</u>. conduct
13. Some neighborhoods <u>have organized special disaster response plans</u>. have organized
14. Certain buildings <u>may be used as gathering places after a disaster</u>. may be used
15. <u>Earthquakes</u> <u>strike without warning</u>.
16. <u>A series of small quakes</u> <u>may precede a large quake</u>.
17. <u>Preparation</u> <u>can save property and lives</u>.
18. ? interrogative
19. . declarative
20. ! exclamatory
21. . (or) ! imperative
22. "Grace, did you see the lightning last night?" asked Zack.
23. "Yes, I was walking outside with Scruffy and Spot, my dogs," said Grace.
24. "They barked, jumped, and growled," she said.
25. ponies   26. lives   27. sheep
28. <u>the</u> tornado touched down in <u>kansas</u> on a warm <u>wednesday</u> in <u>june</u>.
29. <u>brad</u> <u>west</u> and his sisters, <u>olivia</u> and <u>heidi</u>, were at <u>luke's</u> <u>hamburger</u> <u>haven</u>.
30. <u>the</u> <u>morelands'</u> cattle farm on <u>pozer</u> <u>road</u> was miraculously left untouched.

UNIT II

1. <u>The Wolverines</u> <u>will face the Vikings in the playoff game</u>. Wolverines; will face
2. <u>The band members</u> <u>have been practicing all week</u>. members; have been practicing
3. <u>The school band</u> <u>is gathering on the field</u>. band; is gathering
4. The tuba players <u>are wearing</u> Viking helmets. are
5. The drummers <u>have been disguised</u> as wolverines. have been
6. The drummers <u>will chase</u> the tuba players around the field. will
7. is   9. are   11. were
8. are   10. was   12. were

For items 13–15, the second part of each answer will vary.
13. airplanes' engines   16. we're   19. I
14. lawyers' offices   17. haven't   20. He
15. women's coats   18. doesn't   21. he
22. <u>David</u> and <u>Jamie</u> <u>studied</u> music and <u>played</u> together for many years.
23. A <u>parade</u> or a <u>picnic</u> <u>can be</u> an enjoyable event for musicians.
24. A <u>band</u> with horn players <u>adds</u> spirit and <u>encourages</u> clapping.
25. Can <u>you</u> identify all the instruments in the orchestra? Can identify
26. There are <u>violas</u> and <u>cellos</u> in the string section. are
27. <u>They</u> can produce beautiful low tones. can produce
28. took   29. become   30. given

UNIT III

1. Coach Glen <u>had told</u> the <u>team</u> about the upcoming cross-country race.
2. Ari, the team captain, <u>visited</u> <u>Coach Glen</u> in her office.
3. She <u>told</u> <u>Ari</u> about the training schedule.
4. Ari <u>led</u> the <u>team</u> through several conditioning drills.
5. Coach Glen <u>called</u> <u>me</u> into her office.
6. Ari <u>will drive</u> <u>us</u> to the game.
7. Brett <u>led</u> <u>them</u> in a series of exercises.
8. We, practiced, soccer   10. goalie, hurt, ankle
9. team, won, games   11. team, scored, goals
12. Ari kicked the ball <u>toward the goal</u>.
13. The goalie made a futile dive <u>for the</u> <u>ball</u>.
14. The crowd <u>in the</u> far <u>stands</u> cheered enthusiastically.
15. I   16. her, me   17. them   18. us
19. compound personal   21. demonstrative
20. interrogative   22. interrogative
23. Roy brought his chessboard to the park.
24. He challenged Anna to a match, and she accepted.
25. First she defeated him, and then he defeated her.
26. <u>every</u> <u>july</u> there is a pogo stick exhibition in <u>winslow</u> <u>park</u>.
27. <u>wasn't</u> <u>ms.</u> <u>tanaka</u> planning to hop across the <u>united</u> <u>states</u>?
28. <u>yes</u>, she had begun her journey in <u>sarasota</u>, <u>florida</u>.
29. "<u>my</u> favorite hobby is mountain biking," Mari said to Lois.
30. Lois told Mari that she had never ridden a mountain bike.

UNIT IV

1. Some <u>trains</u> <u>can carry</u> (passengers) at very high speeds.
2. Overhead <u>wires</u> <u>supply</u> the (electricity) for these trains.
3. <u>I</u> <u>bought</u> a (ticket) to Chicago.
4. valuable   7. sel-fish   10. lad-der
5. listen   8. X
6. absence   9. X

For items 11–13, answers will vary.
11. drān   12. blŏk   13. kƏn-sist´
14. shrill (whistle); sleek (train)
15. crowded (station); weary (commuters); uncomfortable (commuters)
16. small (child); elderly (engineer)
17. Pablo's (bicycle)   18. his (helmet)
19. instructor's (advice)
20–22. hard, steady, cool, soft, wet

23. lay	25. lying	27. us	29. flew
24. laid	26. I	28. us	30. seen

UNIT V

1. they're   3. she'd   5. whose
2. you'll   4. who's   6. It's
7. skillfully (pruned)   10. capable, adjective
8. sometimes (works)   11. delicious, adjective
9. tomorrow (will prune)   12. expertly, adverb
13. Tanya mowed the lawn <u>yesterday</u>. mowed, verb
14. Sam worked <u>nearby</u> in the flower garden. worked, verb
15. Sam's roses are <u>extremely</u> beautiful. beautiful, adjective
16. great, greatly   17. clearly, clear   18. good, well
19. "<u>margaret</u>, do you make deliveries to many <u>north american</u> cities?" asked <u>tomás</u>.
20. "<u>yes</u>, we've shipped our products to <u>miami</u>, <u>florida</u>, and <u>montreal</u>, <u>quebec</u>," replied <u>margaret</u>.
21. "<u>we've</u> also made deliveries in <u>vancouver</u>, <u>british columbia</u> and <u>san diego</u>, <u>california</u>," she said.
22. here   25. Pat and I   28. May
23. like   26. It's   29. taught
24. she   27. You're   30. bought

UNIT VI

1. The turtle's home is a large rock <u>under the bridge</u>. rock
2. A bench <u>on the lake shore</u> is a good observation spot. bench
3. The tree <u>behind the bench</u> provides shade. tree
4. Two owls made a nest <u>inside our barn</u>. made
5. One owl flew <u>across the yard</u>. flew
6. It probably was hunting <u>for mice</u>. was hunting
7. Owls (hunt) prey <u>at night</u>. adverb
8. They (glide) <u>in silence</u>. adverb
9. The (owls) <u>in our barn</u> control the rodent population. adjective
10. from   14. there   18. very
11. between   15. ever   19. nice
12. in   16. should have
13. went, and   17. sorrowfully
20. Dogs are wonderful <u>pets</u>.   21. Retrievers are <u>friendly</u>.
22. My dog is a <u>poodle</u>.
23. "<u>the april</u> edition of *national geographic* has an article about peregrine falcons," said <u>marta</u>.
24. "<u>does</u> it mention a group in <u>idaho</u> that is trying to help the falcons survive?" asked <u>tyree</u>.
25. "<u>yes</u>, and it also tells about a famous falcon in <u>baltimore</u> named <u>beauregard</u>," said <u>marta</u>.
26. <u>one</u> ornithologist said that some falcons hunt near the city's new baseball park.
27-30. Answers may vary.

     I work at the animal shelter two days a week. Between you and me, people aren't always responsible pet owners. Many people buy exotic pets when they're young and cute. When the pets get bigger, they abandon them. Don't ever buy a pet unless you understand its needs and are prepared to care for it.

UNIT VII

For items 1–5, answers may vary.
1. Because I enjoy cooking, I often invite my friends for dinner.
2. Tonight I'm going to prepare paella or gazpacho.
3. I can't decide what to cook until I've seen what ingredients look the freshest.
4. Ouch   7. throw, threw   10. makes
5. Sorry   8. begin, begun   11. ate
6. went, going   9. recommended   12. will order
13. Sam and Irma <u>had invited</u> friends to breakfast. past perfect
14. None of their guests <u>have arrived</u> yet. present perfect
15. By midday, Sam and Irma probably <u>will have eaten</u>. future perfect
16. are, plural   19. are   22. fragment
17. brings, singular   20. buy   23. comma splice
18. want, singular   21. do   24. run-on
25. "<u>lily</u> has the skills of a professional chef," said <u>grant</u>.
26. "<u>i</u> think she should open her own restaurant in <u>cambridge</u>, <u>massachusetts</u>," said <u>watty</u>.
27. "<u>do</u> you think she would serve pancakes, waffles, or omelets?" asked <u>ella</u>.
28. I <u>like</u> Ethiopian cuisine. present
29. Last month we <u>ate</u> at an Ethiopian restaurant. past
30. I <u>will take</u> you there sometime. future

UNIT VIII

1. overhead   2. bumpy   3. end   4. break
5. "Basketball," Steve said eagerly, "is my favorite sport."
6. He said, "When I made the team, my dad said, 'You should be proud of yourself!'"
7. "Practice," Steve continued, "takes up a lot of my time."
8. hair   10. blew   12. adverb   14. preposition
9. roll   11. steak   13. noun   15. verb
16. The <u>festival</u> <u>attracted</u> people from all over the city. people
17. <u>Floats</u> <u>filled</u> the street during the parade. street
18. <u>Booths</u> along the sidewalk <u>served</u> many kinds of food. food
19. spicier   20. best   21. more complicated
22–26. Answers will vary.

<student's address>
<today's date>

Ms. S. A. Nantauk
Nantauk Interactive
444 DeLargo St.
San Francisco, CA 94117

Dear Ms. Nantauk:

     Please send me a catalog of your company's products. Thank you very much.

         Sincerely,
         <student's signature>

27–30. Answers may vary.
     André and I want to learn how to repair motorcycles. That shop on Wilson Avenue offers a night course for a small fee. We signed up immediately when we heard about it. This opportunity couldn't have come at a better time.

Answer Keys—Achievement Tests

UNIT I

1. yes   2. no   3. no   4. yes
5. <u>Abraham Lincoln</u> was born in a <u>cabin</u> in <u>Kentucky</u>.
6. He was born in the <u>month</u> of <u>February</u>.
7. <u>President's Day</u> honors <u>Abraham Lincoln</u> and <u>George Washington</u>.
8. This <u>holiday</u> is celebrated with <u>ceremonies</u> throughout the <u>United States</u>.
9. <u>Lincoln's family</u> moved to Indiana in 1816.
10. <u>Life</u> was rough and dangerous on the Indiana frontier.
11. <u>Wild animals</u> posed a constant threat.
12. Several fine writers <u>have written biographies of Lincoln</u>. have written
13. Lincoln <u>had less than a year of formal education</u>. had
14. He <u>taught himself reading and writing</u>. taught
15. <u>Young Abe Lincoln</u> <u>had a keen mind</u>.
16. <u>He</u> <u>became a lawyer in 1836</u>.
17. <u>This son of the frontier</u> <u>entered politics several years later</u>.
18. . declarative   20. ? interrogative
19. ! exclamatory   21. . imperative
22. "Do you admire Abraham Lincoln, Alison?" asked Duke.
23. "Yes, he guided the nation during the Civil War, its darkest hour," Alison replied.
24. "He led with wisdom, intelligence, and strength," she continued.
25. lives   26. enemies   27. children
28. <u>robert</u> E. Lee surrendered to <u>ulysses</u> S. <u>grant</u> on <u>april</u> 9, 1865.
29. <u>the</u> surrender took place in <u>appomattox, virginia</u>.
30. <u>president lincoln</u> was assassinated in <u>washington</u>, D.C., on <u>april</u> 14, 1865.

UNIT II

1. <u>Many wild creatures</u> <u>are found in cities</u>. creatures, are found
2. <u>Raccoons</u> <u>live quite comfortably in urban parks</u>. Raccoons, live
3. <u>Opossums</u> <u>have been seen in city neighborhoods, too</u>. opossums, have been seen
4. Migrating birds <u>have stopped</u> at that pond. have
5. I <u>have been watching</u> a pair of wood ducks. have been
6. They <u>will continue</u> their journey soon. will
7. are   9. is   11. was
8. are   10. were   12. were

In items 13–15, the second part of each answer will vary.

13. men's raincoats   15. officer's badge
14. raccoons' masks
16. you'll   18. can't   20. they
17. I'm   19. I   21. I
22. <u>Raccoons</u> and <u>opossums</u> <u>are</u> nocturnal.
23. <u>They</u> <u>prowl</u> at night and <u>search</u> for food in the areas near their homes.
24. My <u>neighbors</u> and <u>I</u> <u>cover</u> our trash cans and <u>close</u> the pet doors.
25. There are many ugly <u>holes</u> in my lawn. are
26. <u>They</u> are the work of raccoons. are
27. Do the <u>raccoons</u> dig for roots and insects? Do dig
28. began   29. grown   30. done

UNIT III

1. Captain Drotning <u>bought</u> a <u>book</u> about figure drawing.
2. She <u>practiced</u> <u>drawing</u> after work every day.
3. She <u>noticed</u> real <u>improvement</u> in her work after three weeks.
4. Myra, Captain Drotning's cousin, <u>is studying</u> <u>design</u> at night.
5. Rachel <u>called</u> <u>me</u> on the telephone.
6. She <u>will meet</u> <u>you</u> at the book store.
7. My art teacher <u>invited</u> <u>us</u> to her opening.
8. We, will buy, book
9. Leonardo, created, paintings
10. He, designed, machines
11. He, sketched, idea
12. This drawing <u>of a human</u> <u>shoulder</u> is quite accurate.
13. Leonardo studied anatomy <u>in great</u> <u>detail</u>.
14. That drawing shows his idea <u>for a moveable</u> <u>bridge</u>.
15. I   16. us   17. them   18. her, me
19. compound personal   21. demonstrative
20. interrogative   22. interrogative
23. Gerald brought his paint set to school.
24. Susan asked him to help her on a project.
25. She mixed paints for him, and then he mixed paints for her.
26. <u>leonardo</u> was born near <u>florence, italy</u>.
27. <u>didn't</u> <u>leonardo</u> live in <u>tours, france</u>, later in his life?
28. <u>yes</u>, he lived there, and he also lived in <u>milan, italy</u>.
29. "<u>my</u> favorite artist is Michelangelo," I said to Rachel.
30. <u>she</u> told me that she admires his work, too.

UNIT IV

1. Ricardo's <u>uncle</u> <u>found</u> some old (pottery) at a construction site.
2. His <u>discovery</u> <u>excited</u> the local (historians).
3. <u>Ricardo</u> <u>is studying</u> ancient (civilizations) in school.
4. every   7. wel-come   10. log-ger
5. curious   8. X
6. chief   9. X

For items 11–13, answers will vary.

11. dis-plā′   12. un′yən   13. blām
14. small (shards), blue (bowl)
15. three (arrowheads), shiny (arrowheads), deep (ditch)
16. interesting (artifacts), local (museum)
17. <u>Ricardo's</u> (classes)   18. <u>His</u> (professors)
19. <u>week's</u> (assignments), <u>their</u> (evenings)
20–22. new, Eager, distant, huge, several
23. lay   25. lain   27. We   29. drawn
24. lying   26. himself   28. us   30. took

UNIT V

1. he'd   3. what's   5. You're
2. you're   4. there's   6. It's

7. rapidly (dropped)   10. successful, adjective
8. sometimes (cause)   11. impressive, adjective
9. Soon (will freeze)   12. often, adverb
13. The explorers <u>quickly</u> constructed a snow hut. constructed, verb
14. The dogs remained <u>outside</u>. remained, verb
15. Sled dogs have <u>incredibly</u> thick coats. thick, adjective
16. good, well   17. near, nearly   18. slight, slightly
19. "<u>deanna</u>, did that story take place in <u>sitka</u>, <u>alaska</u>?" asked <u>rick</u>.
20. "<u>no</u>, the setting was <u>siberia</u>," <u>deanna</u> replied.
21. "<u>the</u> movie was filmed in <u>canada</u>, <u>russia</u>, and <u>alaska</u>," she continued.
22. there   25. your   28. written
23. he   26. it's   29. May
24. like   27. LaMont and I   30. teach

UNIT VI

1. The Air Force is one branch <u>of the armed forces</u>. branch
2. That plane <u>on the ground</u> is an F-16. plane
3. The stripes <u>on this insignia</u> show rank. stripes
4. My brother Derek joined the Air Force <u>in 1992</u>. joined
5. He trained <u>at Lackland Air Force Base</u>. trained
6. Those recruits will learn <u>about military life</u>. will learn
7. Derek (studied) aircraft repair <u>for four years</u>. adverb
8. Now he (lives) <u>in Hawaii</u>. adverb
9. (Mechanics) <u>in the Air Force</u> are highly skilled. adjective
10. between   13. there   16. have   19. hoarsely
11. of   14. he   17. very
12. in   15. ever   18. loud
20. An F-15 Eagle is <u>loud</u>!
21. My brother is a <u>mechanic</u>.
22. His job seems <u>fascinating</u>.
23. "<u>have</u> you ever heard of <u>jacqueline</u> <u>cochran</u>?" <u>derek</u> asked.
24. "<u>yes</u>, she was a famous aviation pioneer," said <u>dierdre</u>.
25. "<u>she</u> led a team of <u>american</u> women pilots during <u>world</u> <u>war</u> II," <u>dierdre</u> continued.
26. <u>derek</u> explained that the women flew within the <u>united</u> <u>states</u> but not in <u>europe</u>.
27–30. Answers may vary slightly.

Susan works in the community garden two weekends each month. Between you and me, that job isn't easy to do. There are always weeds to pull, and the compost has to be turned every day if it's going to become good fertilizer. I wouldn't ever sign up for that job. If you like to spend your time outside, it might be a good job for you.

UNIT VII

For items 1–5, answers may vary.
1. We will stop at the Grand Canyon or Tombstone today.

2. Although Arizona is mostly desert, some places are heavily forested.
3. We saw the Painted Desert when we visited Arizona.
4. Ouch   7. flew, flying   10. took
5. Help   8. teach, taught, taught   11. brought
6. sing, sung 9. hiked   12. will develop
13. have planned, present perfect
14. had been, past perfect
15. will have seen, future perfect
16. cover, plural   19. live   22. fragment
17. need, singular   20. inhabit   23. comma splice
18. are, plural   21. are   24. run-on
25. "<u>isn't</u> <u>hoover</u> <u>dam</u> on the <u>colorado</u> <u>river</u>?" asked <u>hugh</u>.
26. "<u>it</u> supplies electric power to <u>nevada</u>, <u>arizona</u>, and <u>california</u>," said <u>raul</u>.
27. "<u>tucson</u>, <u>arizona</u>, was once a frontier fort," <u>i</u> added.
28. Arizona <u>became</u> a state in 1912. past
29. I <u>see</u> rock paintings on that wall. present
30. On Tuesday we <u>will visit</u> Tucson. future

UNIT VIII

1. discover   2. frighten   3. blame   4. destroy
5. "The stars," Leo said, "have always fascinated me."
6. He said, "When I asked my parents for a telescope, they asked, 'Will you really use it?'"
7. "That telescope," he continued, "has been invaluable."
8. stare   10. sent   12. noun   14. preposition
9. flour   11. brake   13. adjective 15. verb
16. <u>Galileo</u> <u>studied</u> the (sky) in the 1600s.
17. His <u>observations</u> of the planets <u>confirmed</u> Copernicus's (conclusions.)
18. This great <u>scientist</u> <u>used</u> a simple (telescope) in his studies.
19. better   20. brighter   21. most visible
22–26. Answers may vary.

<student's address>

<today's date>

Althea Anderson
Night Sky Productions
1004 Aquarius Rd.
Columbus, OH 43215

Dear Ms. Anderson:

Please send me a copy of the free star map offered in the newspaper. Thank you very much.

Yours truly,

<student's signature>

27–30. Answers may vary.

Leo and I have a telescope. We bought it at that flea market. It didn't cost much, and it works very well. We're carefully mapping the constellations. We couldn't have started this project without a telescope.

Individual Record-Keeping Form   Student's Name _____

DIAGNOSTIC AND ACHIEVEMENT TESTS

	DIAGNOSTIC (Perfect Score: 30)	ACHIEVEMENT (Perfect Score: 30)	OBSERVATIONS
Unit I			
Unit II			
Unit III			
Unit IV			
Unit V			
Unit VI			
Unit VII			
Unit VIII			

Overall Assessment: _____

_____

_____

ORAL LANGUAGE OBSERVATION CHECKLIST

Listening   (Observe student's ability to: follow oral directions; understand passages read aloud; respond to questions; retain information presented orally.)

Date	Task	Observation

Speaking   (Observe student's ability to: use correct syntax; use standard English when appropriate; explain ideas or processes; summarize new concepts; retell stories.)

Date	Task	Observation

Overall Assessment: _____

_____

_____

Writing Rubric and Evaluation Checklists

Using the Writing Rubric. This rubric summarizes general characteristics of compositions written by students of varying levels of proficiency. Use this rubric in conjunction with the Checklists for Evaluating Composition Lessons, which appear on the next four pages, to help you evaluate students' writing.

Superior (4)

- Purpose, task, and audience (if specified) are addressed.
- Composition structure shows an understanding of the structure of the writing form.
- Ideas are well organized and elaborated upon in detail.
- Sentences are complete and correctly written.
- Capitalization and punctuation are used correctly.
- Nearly all words are spelled correctly.

Good (3)

- Purpose, task, and audience (if specified) are addressed fairly effectively.
- Composition structure shows some sense of the structure of the writing form.
- Ideas are organized, but not elaborated upon; or, writing exhibits good use of elaboration and detail, but ideas are not clearly organized.
- Most sentences are complete and correctly written.
- Most capitalization and punctuation are used correctly.
- Most words are spelled correctly.

Average (2)

- Task, purpose, and audience (if specified) are addressed to some extent.
- Organization of ideas is not apparent; little elaboration or detail is used.
- Shows some understanding of the structure of the writing form, but may have omitted key elements (such as a topic sentence or a conclusion).
- Writing may lack unity and focus; may contain nonsequiturs or sentences off the topic.
- Some fragments, run-ons, or comma splices may appear.
- Structure of some sentences is awkward or simplistic.
- A number of errors in capitalization, punctuation, and spelling occur.

Working Toward Improvement (1)

- Task, purpose, and audience (if specified) are not addressed.
- Writing lacks organization and focus: sentences may ramble; ideas seem unconnected; some sentences do not address topic.
- Writing shows little or no understanding of the structure or purpose of the writing form.
- Writing shows limited or no awareness of paragraph structure.
- Writing shows limited control of language; many sentences are incomplete or improperly structured.
- Writing contains many errors in grammar, usage, mechanics, and spelling.

Using the Evaluation Checklists. Duplicate a set of checklists for each student. Use them to assist you in evaluating each student's written work over the course of the year. To evaluate each writing lesson, check the box next to each item the student has completed correctly. Then add the checkmarks and record the score on the line. In addition to this score, give each writing assignment an overall score based on the Writing Rubric.

Checklists for Evaluating Composition Lessons

Student's Name_____

Use check marks to indicate items answered correctly and objectives fulfilled.

LESSON 10: Writing a Product Endorsement

Read a Product Endorsement

Item   Correct Response
- ❑ 1.   The first sentence should be underlined.
- ❑ 2.   An X should appear by sentences 2–8.
- ❑ 3.   *sturdier; better; higher quality; less*
- ❑ 4.   compare the model with the other brands for quality, reliability, sound, and price
- ❑ 5.   The last part of the last sentence should be underlined.
- ❑ 6.   Possible response: a student
- ❑ 7.   Possible responses: the price; the reliability; the durability

Write a Product Endorsement Check whether the student has
- ❑ selected a familiar product as a topic.
- ❑ listed reasons for endorsing the product.
- ❑ evaluated the first draft critically, and revised it.

Evaluating the Product Endorsement Check whether the student has
- ❑ named the product in the first sentence.
- ❑ stated and endorsed an opinion in the first part of the paragraph.
- ❑ restated the opinion and summed up the reasons in the last sentence.
- ❑ used language and reasons that appeal to the audience.
- ❑ used comparative words.
- ❑ used correct capitalization, spelling, and punctuation.

Perfect Score: 16 Student's Score: _____ Rating Scale **4 3 2 1** (*See* Rubric p. 61)

LESSON 21: Writing a Biography

Read a Biography

Item   Correct Response
- ❑ 1.   **when**—*1901*; **where**—*in the small village of Bari, in southern Italy*
- ❑ 2.   An X should appear next to each detail showing the order of events.
- ❑ 3.   Possible responses: Mario escaped from Italy to America; he worked for the U.S. Steel Company in San Francisco; he retired to Santa Cruz
- ❑ 4.   The last sentence should be underlined.
- ❑ 5.   Possible responses: *Mario spoke out against Mussolini's strict regime; it was very important to him that his sons get good educations*

Write a Biography Check whether the student has
- ❑ selected a familiar person as a topic.
- ❑ obtained details about the person's life and experiences.
- ❑ evaluated the first draft and made revisions to improve it.

Evaluating the Biography Check whether the student has
- ❑ introduced the person at the beginning.
- ❑ described important events in time order.
- ❑ included specific dates and places.
- ❑ started with the time and place of birth.
- ❑ ended by describing the person now, if alive, or the date and place of death.
- ❑ used correct capitalization and punctuation.
- ❑ spelled most words, including place names, correctly.

Perfect Score: 15 Student's Score: _____ Rating Scale **4 3 2 1** (*See* Rubric p. 61)

Student's Name _____

Use check marks to indicate items answered correctly and objectives fulfilled.

LESSON 32: Writing a Summary

Read a Summary

Item   *Correct Response*

❑ 1.   The check mark should be by the first sentence.
❑ 2.   Cinque; Roger Baldwin; Martin Van Buren; John Quincy Adams
❑ 3.   Djimon Hounsou; Matthew McConaughey; Nigel Hawthorne; Anthony Hopkins
❑ 4.   The star should be next to the third sentence.
❑ 5.   The second sentence should be underlined.
❑ 6.   The X should be by the last paragraph.

Write a Summary Check whether the student has

❑ chosen a historical movie.
❑ found the information needed to describe the movie.
❑ revised the summary. (Review the first draft and have the student explain how it was revised.)

Evaluating the Summary Check whether the student has

❑ introduced the main facts of the movie in the first sentences (title; director; historical event or figure).
❑ described the events portrayed in the movie, including main characters and actors.
❑ described the theme of the movie in the last paragraph.
❑ begun a new paragraph with each change of idea, place, or time.
❑ used correct capitalization and punctuation.
❑ spelled most words correctly.

Perfect Score: 15 Student's Score: _____ Rating Scale **4 3 2 1** (*See* Rubric p. 61)

LESSON 43: Writing a History Report

Read a History Report

Item   *Correct Response*

❑ 1.   The first sentence should be underlined.
❑ 2.   Paragraphs 2–4 are the paragraphs of information.
❑ 3.   Lucretia Mott; Elizabeth Stanton; Susan B. Anthony; Lucy Stone; Henry Blackwell
❑ 4.   The star should be by the last paragraph.
❑ 5.   three

Write a History Report Check whether the student has

❑ understood that the writing process is broken down into six distinct steps.
❑ gathered information on the chosen topic.
❑ organized the facts in an outline.
❑ understood the purpose of a first draft.
❑ revised the first draft to improve it.

Evaluating the History Report Check whether the student has

❑ begun the report with an introductory paragraph.
❑ presented facts about the topic in paragraphs of information.
❑ written about events in sequence.
❑ used formal language and punctuated it correctly.
❑ spelled most words correctly.
❑ used and listed correctly at least two reference sources.

Perfect Score: 16 Student's Score: _____ Rating Scale **4 3 2 1** (*See* Rubric p. 61)

Student's Name _____

Use check marks to indicate items answered correctly and objectives fulfilled.

LESSON 54: Writing a News Article

Read a News Article

Item — Correct Response

❑ 1.   a Special Olympics competition
❑ 2.   Roosevelt High School
❑ 3.   March 14–16
❑ 4.   forty-seven athletes and many community volunteers
❑ 5.   The athletes competed in swimming, basketball, and track. The community volunteers helped the athletes before, during, and after the events.
❑ 6.   yes (*The Special Olympics was a great experience for everyone involved; The community looks forward to another Special Olympics in March of next year*)

Write a News Article Check whether the student has
❑ selected an event as a topic.
❑ used the organizer to list important facts.
❑ revised the article, adding improvements.

Evaluating the News Article Check whether the student has
❑ answered the questions *Who, Where, When, What,* and *Why* or *How*?
❑ described the correct order of events.
❑ included a title.
❑ used correct capitalization and punctuation.
❑ spelled most words correctly.

Perfect Score: 14   Student's Score: _____   Rating Scale **4 3 2 1** (*See* Rubric p. 61)

LESSON 65: Writing a Descriptive Composition

Read a Descriptive Composition

Item — Correct Response

❑ 1.   The check mark should be by the first sentence.
❑ 2.   it is divided into about a dozen cubicles by blue partitions
❑ 3.   Possible responses: *glass door . . . ; very large room . . . ; a dozen cubicles . . . ; Blue partitions . . . ; The offices were small and looked messy . . .*
❑ 4.   Possible responses: comfortable; informal; friendly
❑ 5.   an editor; a designer; some programmers
❑ 6.   The last sentence should be underlined.

Write a Descriptive Composition Check whether the student has
❑ visited a workplace of their choice.
❑ listed the information needed to describe the visit.
❑ revised the first draft.

Evaluating the Descriptive Composition Check whether the student has
❑ identified the place in the first sentence.
❑ described features of the place and its character.
❑ described what was done and observed, in sequence order.
❑ described the people that were met.
❑ used adjectives and prepositional phrases.
❑ ended the description with an overall impression.
❑ used correct capitalization, punctuation, and spelling.

Perfect Score: 16   Student's Score: _____   Rating Scale **4 3 2 1** (*See* Rubric p. 61)

Student's Name _____

Use check marks to indicate items answered correctly and objectives fulfilled.

LESSON 76: Writing a Compare/Contrast Essay

Read a Compare/Contrast Essay

Item   Correct Response
- ❏ 1.   The third sentence should be underlined.
- ❏ 2.   The first sentence in the second paragraph, and the first sentence in the third paragraph should be underlined.
- ❏ 3.   The star should be by the second paragraph.
- ❏ 4.   The X should be by the third paragraph.
- ❏ 5.   Possible responses: *on the other hand; unlike*
- ❏ 6.   The check mark should be next to the last paragraph. The last two sentences should be underlined.

Write a Compare/Contrast Essay Check whether the student has
- ❏ chosen two people that have both differences and similarities.
- ❏ used the plan diagram to list similarities and differences.
- ❏ revised the essay. (Review the first draft and have students explain how it was revised.)

Evaluating the Compare/Contrast Essay Check whether the student has
- ❏ introduced the characters in the first paragraph.
- ❏ described their similarities in the second paragraph.
- ❏ described their differences in the third paragraph.
- ❏ summed up the observations in the final paragraph.
- ❏ used a topic sentence in each paragraph.
- ❏ used correct punctuation, capitalization, and spelling.

Perfect Score: 15 Student's Score: _____ Rating Scale **4 3 2 1** (*See* Rubric p. 61)

LESSON 87: Writing a Personal Narrative

Read a Personal Narrative

Item   Correct Response
- ❏ 1.   Any one of the following pronouns should be circled: *I, me, my, mine, we, our.*
- ❏ 2.   that he knew how to drive an automatic car, and thought standard transmission would be easy to learn
- ❏ 3.   In the middle he describes his first attempt at driving stick shift.
- ❏ 4.   He ends it by describing what he learned from the experience.
- ❏ 5.   Possible responses: *first stop; finally; eventually*
- ❏ 6.   Possible responses describing narrator: *I'm doing great!; Things were going fine . . . ; I managed to make my way home just fine . . . ; I beamed triumphantly . . . ; I was sure Dad was impressed . . .*
Possible responses describing his father: *Dad yelled; he looked very pale*
- ❏ 7.   The last two sentences should be underlined.

Write a Personal Narrative Check whether the student has
- ❏ understood that the writing process includes five distinct steps.
- ❏ brainstormed topic ideas and selected a topic from among them.
- ❏ listed the events in sequence before writing.
- ❏ understood the purpose of a first draft.
- ❏ revised the first draft, and made a clean final copy.

Evaluating the Personal Narrative Check whether the student has
- ❏ described a personal experience using the first-person voice.
- ❏ demonstrated correct use of the personal pronouns *I, me, mine, my, we,* and *our.*
- ❏ included a beginning, a middle, and an end in the narrative.
- ❏ made the setting (time and place) clear to the reader.
- ❏ used sequence words to indicate order of events.
- ❏ described feelings as well as events.
- ❏ used conversational language, including dialogue.
- ❏ begun a new paragraph with each change of speaker, idea, time, or place.
- ❏ used capitalization and punctuation correctly.

Perfect Score: 21 Student's Score: _____ Rating Scale **4 3 2 1** (*See* Rubric p. 61)

Answer Keys for Student Lesson Pages

Lesson 1

PART I

1. yes	5. no	9. no	13. no
2. yes	6. yes	10. yes	
3. no	7. no	11. yes	
4. yes	8. yes	12. yes	

PART II

Answers will vary.

Lesson 2

PART I

1. (?) interrogative	9. (.) declarative
2. (?) interrogative	10. (.) imperative
3. (!) exclamatory	11. (!) exclamatory
4. (.) declarative	12. (.) declarative
5. (?) interrogative	13. (?) interrogative
6. (?) interrogative	14. (.) imperative
7. (.) declarative	15. (!) exclamatory
8. (!) exclamatory	16. (?) interrogative

PART II

Answers will vary.

Lesson 3

PART I

1. A great many people
2. Boots, poles, and skis
3. Skiers from many countries
4. The games of the Winter Olympics
5. Large crowds
6. These events
7. A new and exciting event
8. The skiers
9. Contestants in cross-country races
10. Bjorn Daehlie of Norway
11. That victory
12. The downhill races and the slalom contests
13. The slope for the downhill
14. Courage, skill, and speed
15. Hanni Wenzel and Marielle Goitschel

PART II

Answers will vary.

Lesson 4

PART I

1. was "The Celebrated Jumping Frog of Calaveras County," was
2. was named Jim Smiley, was named
3. had a favorite pastime, had
4. would bet on anything, would bet
5. made bets on horses, dogs, doodlebugs, and frogs, made
6. had a frog by the name of Dan'l Webster, had
7. would enter his frog in jumping contests, would enter
8. won all the contests in the county, won
9. came to town one day, came
10. needed a frog for a contest with Dan'l Webster, needed
11. went to the pond for a frog for the stranger, went
12. left Dan'l Webster alone with the stranger, left
13. won the contest easily, won
14. had filled poor Dan'l Webster with buckshot, had filled

PART II

Answers will vary.

Lesson 5

PART I

1. Smallpox is a contagious disease.
2. Thousands of people caught smallpox every year until recently.
3. Egyptian pharaohs became ill and died from it long ago.
4. Queen Elizabeth I lost her hair as a result of smallpox.
5. That powerful leader wore red wigs after her illness.
6. George Washington had smallpox scars on his face.
7. Dr. Edward Jenner struck a blow against smallpox in 1796.
8. His vaccine prevented this illness.
9. The World Health Organization fought smallpox all over the world.
10. Officials announced wonderful news in 1980.
11. The dream of a world free from smallpox had come true.

PART II

Answers will vary.
Synonym Watch: antiseptic—sterilized

Lesson 6

PART I

1. boats, logs
2. People, paddles, boats
3. Ships, Egypt, oars, sails
4. ships, Greeks, oars
5. Vikings, shipbuilders, navigators
6. ships, oars, sails
7. ships, Atlantic Ocean, century
8. type, ship, time, Columbus, caravel
9. sails, speed
10. caravels, fleet, Columbus, America
11. Shipbuilders, United States, clippers
12. 1807, Robert Fulton, steamship, United States
13. ship, *Clermont*, Hudson River, New York City, Albany

14. In 1838 a steamship traveled from Cork, Ireland, to New York in seventeen days.
15. In 1992 an Italian powerboat traveled from Nantucket Island, Massachusetts, to England in under sixty hours.
16. Hyman Rickover helped develop the atomic submarine after World War II.
17. He was an officer in the United States Navy.

Lesson 7

1. creature	8. fish	15. germ
2. ocean	9. floors	16. women
3. bodies	10. bridges	17. knives
4. eel	11. shelves	18. catches
5. foot	12. injury	19. decks
6. tooth	13. lives	
7. jaw	14. cries	

Near Misses: First sentence: *bazaar* should be spelled *bizarre*.

Lesson 8

PART I

1. "Who wrote *Poor Richard's Almanac*, Dana?" asked Kris.
2. "Thomas Jefferson, our third president, wrote it," answered Dana.
3. "No, Jefferson didn't write it," said Tanisha.
4. Tanisha said, "Ben Franklin, a scientist and humorist, wrote that almanac."
5. "I can tell you about other early American almanacs, Kris," said Dana.
6. "Benjamin Banneker, an African American, wrote several almanacs," Dana continued.
7. "Wasn't Banneker a clockmaker, a surveyor, and an inventor?" asked Tanisha.
8. "Yes, and he was also an astronomer, a mathematician, and a farmer," Dana replied.
9. "Dana, what facts were in Banneker's almanacs?" asked Kris.
10. "Banneker included tide tables, weather forecasts, and eclipse dates," said Dana.
11. Kris said, "Dana, I remember reading about Benjamin Banneker."
12. "He helped plan our national capital, Washington, D.C.," she explained.

PART II

Answers will vary.
Odd Word Out: *rototiller* does not belong; other words could fit in the category "dentistry"; *rototiller* could fit in the category "gardening" or "machines for lawn care."

Lesson 9

PART I

1. <u>on</u> <u>sunday</u>, <u>june</u> 26, 1955, an unusual museum was opened in <u>oklahoma</u>.
2. <u>the</u> <u>national</u> <u>cowboy</u> <u>hall</u> of <u>fame</u> and <u>western</u> <u>heritage</u> <u>center</u> is its name.
3. <u>this</u> museum is in <u>oklahoma</u> <u>city</u> on a high bluff called <u>persimmon</u> <u>hill</u>.
4. <u>it</u> honors famous <u>americans</u> of the western region.
5. <u>all</u> fifty states of the <u>united</u> <u>states</u> are represented there, however.
6. <u>in</u> the museum are paintings by <u>frederic</u> <u>remington</u>.
7. <u>he</u> and <u>charles</u> <u>m.</u> <u>russell</u> were famous western painters.
8. <u>the</u> list of honored persons includes <u>general</u> <u>sam</u> <u>houston</u> of <u>texas</u>.
9. <u>will</u> <u>rogers</u>, the <u>oklahoma</u> humorist, was chosen for the list.
10. <u>president</u> <u>theodore</u> <u>roosevelt</u>, who once worked as a rancher, is also in the group.
11. <u>among</u> the women on the list is <u>sacagawea</u>.
12. <u>she</u> guided <u>lewis</u> and <u>clark</u> on their journey to the <u>pacific</u> <u>ocean</u> in 1805.
13. <u>another</u> honored person is <u>sequoyah</u>, who created the <u>cherokee</u> alphabet.
14. <u>buffalo</u> <u>bill</u> <u>cody</u>, a famous performer, is honored, too.

PART II

15. J. T. Horning and I visited the museum one Saturday last summer.
16. He and I saw the saddle used by Gary Cooper in some of his films.
17. The National Cowboy Hall of Fame honors excellent western heritage films.
18. A movie about the Sioux, <u>Dances with Wolves</u>, won seven Academy Awards in 1990.

Lesson 11

PART I

Answers will vary.

PART II

3. Terry, have you read <u>My Name Is Aram</u>?
4. Yes, I finished reading that novel on Monday, April 20.
5. It was written by William Saroyan, an Armenian American writer, in 1940.
6. Saroyan's books and stories are honest, humorous, and full of positive thinking.

PART III

Answers will vary.

Lesson 12

PART I

1. <u>Another name for this creature is the yeti</u>, name, is
2. <u>Large tracks have been seen in the Himalaya Mountains</u>, tracks, have been seen
3. <u>Many people have looked for this beast</u>, people, have looked
4. <u>Farmers have reported glimpses of it</u>, farmers, have reported
5. <u>These people describe it as half-human and half-ape</u>, people, describe
6. <u>Many local people are afraid of the yeti</u>, people, are
7. <u>Mountain climbers have searched for it</u>, climbers, have searched
8. <u>A British explorer took pictures of huge footprints</u>, explorer, took
9. <u>Several searches have been made for the beast</u>, searches, have been made
10. <u>Nobody has proved the existence of this creature</u>, nobody, has proved
11. <u>The huge tracks may have been bear tracks</u>, tracks, may have been

PART II

Answers will vary.
Odd Word Out: *crevice* does not belong; other words could fit in the category "circulatory system" or "parts of the body"; *crevice* could fit in the category "types of openings."

Lesson 13

PART I

1. <u>must know</u>, must
2. <u>can recognize</u>, can
3. <u>have been called</u>, have been
4. <u>may recognize</u>, may
5. <u>were invented</u>, were
6. <u>was nicknamed</u>, was
7. <u>can be identified</u>, can be
8. <u>have written</u>, have
9. <u>had become</u>, had
10. <u>had advertised</u>, had
11. <u>has become</u>, has
12. <u>has made</u>, has
13. <u>was given</u>, was

PART II

Answers will vary.

Lesson 14

1. is	6. are	11. are	16. is
2. is	7. is	12. are	17. is
3. are	8. is	13. is	18. are
4. are	9. are	14. are	
5. is	10. are	15. is	

Lesson 15

1. were	5. were	9. were	13. were
2. was	6. were	10. was	14. was
3. was	7. were	11. was	15. was
4. were	8. was	12. was	16. was

Word Whiz: biology, geology, anthropology

Lesson 16

PART I

The second part of each answer will vary.

1. women's	7. radio's	11. men's
2. performers'	8. oxen's	12. Bess's
3. doctors'	9. Lucy's	13. wolf's
4. ocean's	10. crowd's	14. boy's
5. artists'		
6. car's		

PART II

15. can't	20. I've	25. she's
16. you're	21. haven't	26. I'm
17. doesn't	22. it's	27. isn't
18. you'll	23. weren't	28. don't
19. we're	24. won't	

Odd Word Out: *meridian* does not belong; other words fit in the category "rocks" or "geology"; *meridian* fits in the category "geography" or "longitude"

Lesson 17

PART I

1. I	3. He, she	5. I	7. She
2. He	4. They	6. They, I	

PART II

8. she	10. he	12. We
9. he	11. I	13. he

Connecting Meanings: convene—meet in a group; concur—agree; conspire—secretly plan something illegal together. Check students' sentences to be sure they have used *convene, concur,* and *conspire* correctly.

Lesson 18

PART I

1. <u>California</u>, <u>Washington</u>, <u>are</u>
2. <u>Lava</u>, <u>ash</u>, <u>poured</u>, <u>roared</u>
3. <u>It</u> <u>has been</u>, <u>has produced</u>
4. <u>mud</u>, <u>water</u>, <u>bubble</u>, <u>spit</u>
5. <u>Visitors</u>, <u>ski</u>, <u>snowshoe</u>
6. <u>peak</u>, <u>showed</u>
7. <u>ash</u>, <u>rocks</u>, <u>exploded</u>, <u>formed</u>
8. <u>Eruptions</u>, <u>flattened</u>, <u>destroyed</u>
9. <u>Alaska</u>, <u>Hawaii</u>, <u>have</u>
10. <u>Hawaiians</u>, <u>tourists</u>, <u>hear</u>, <u>see</u>
11. <u>Fishers</u>, <u>hikers</u>, <u>sightseers</u>, <u>come</u>
12. <u>visitors</u>, <u>watch</u>, <u>wonder</u>
13. <u>wonders</u>, <u>mystify</u>, <u>interest</u>

PART II

Answers will vary.
Antonym Watch: massive—tiny

Lesson 19

PART I

1. <u>skywriters</u>, are
2. <u>skywriter</u>, must be
3. <u>skywriter</u>, must be
4. <u>type</u>, is
5. <u>plane</u>, must be built
6. <u>letters</u>, are made
7. <u>letters</u>, are written
8. <u>trail</u>, is released

PART II

9. she, does write
10. she, must study
11. letter, does take
12. letter, is
13. she, can read
14. wind, has spoiled
15. skywriters, do misspell
16. misspellings, have been

Lesson 20

PART I

1. spent
2. took
3. seen
4. gone
5. taken
6. become
7. began
8. spent
9. bought
10. grew
11. made
12. began
13. chose
14. built
15. took
16. made
17. seen
18. given
19. become
20. wrote

PART II

Answers will vary.

Lesson 22

PARTS I AND II

Answers will vary.

PART III

7. is
8. were
9. was
10. were
11. was
12. are

PART IV

Answers will vary.

PART V

17. began
18. grown
19. rose
20. gave
21. become
22. found

Lesson 23

PART I

1. have gained, <u>fame</u>, <u>fortune</u>
2. ran, <u>shop</u>
3. brewed, <u>remedies</u>
4. planned, <u>program</u>
5. wanted, <u>powders</u>, <u>tonics</u>, <u>creams</u>
6. bought, <u>space</u>
7. offered, <u>medicines</u>
8. formed, <u>lines</u>
9. <u>was</u> <u>making</u>, <u>money</u>
10. <u>was</u> <u>selling</u>, <u>number</u>

PART II

11. He spent sixteen hours each day at work.
12. Jesse saved money during his first successful years.
13. He did not readily change his habits.
14. Jesse Boot would not drive a car for many years.
15. Until 1904 he rode a horse on visits to his shops.

Lesson 24

PART I

1. had cheated, <u>us</u>
2. notified, <u>Wayne</u>, <u>me</u>
3. had fooled, <u>her</u>
4. had altered, <u>them</u>
5. had counted, <u>them</u>
6. sent, <u>Wayne</u>, <u>me</u>
7. asked, <u>us</u>
8. fooled, <u>Wayne</u>, <u>me</u>
9. informed, <u>manager</u>, <u>us</u>
10. remembered, <u>him</u>
11. could recognize, <u>him</u>
12. spotted, <u>him</u>
13. sent, <u>Vera</u>, <u>me</u>
14. caught, <u>him</u>

PART II

Answers may vary.

15. us
16. me
17. him, me
18. her
19. us
20. me
21. them

Lesson 25

1. I; noticed; story
2. People; celebrate; event
3. friends, relatives; sent; cards
4. article; showed; cards
5. card; showed; woman
6. she; was holding; bouquet
7. woman; held; cluster
8. card; featured; man, woman
9. She, he; were carrying; basket
10. I; like; idea
11. I; could send; cards

Lesson 26

PART I

1. <u>In the 1960s, at home, for her children</u>
2. <u>of her childhood</u>
3. <u>for a party, in Louisiana</u>
4. <u>in this lively music</u>
5. <u>in French</u>
6. <u>of Louisiana Cajuns</u>
7. <u>In her spare time, on her accordion</u>
8. <u>At first, to her children</u>
9. <u>of them, in a zydeco band</u>
10. <u>At 42, in public</u>
11. <u>with her audiences</u>
12. <u>of all ages, to her infectious music</u>
13. <u>At a festival, of Zydeco</u>
14. <u>Since that time, at the Monterey Jazz Festival</u>
15. <u>in recent years</u>
16. <u>in concert</u>
17. <u>on tour</u>
18. <u>of their most-popular albums, *with Queen Ida*</u>

Answers will vary.
Near Misses: Second sentence: *anecdote* should be *antidote*.

Lesson 27

PART I

1. I
2. I
3. She
4. she, I
5. her, me
6. She
7. we
8. us
9. them
10. us
11. me
12. her, me
13. them, us
14. them

PART II

15. I, subject
16. I, subject
17. She, subject
18. she, subject
19. I, subject
20. her, object of preposition
21. me, object of preposition
22. She, subject
23. we, subject
24. us, object of preposition
25. them, direct object
26. us, object of preposition
27. me, direct object
28. her, direct object
29. me, direct object
30. them, object of preposition
31. us, object of preposition

Lesson 28

1. compound personal
2. interrogative
3. demonstrative
4. compound personal
5. demonstrative
6. interrogative
7. demonstrative
8. interrogative
9. demonstrative
10. interrogative
11. demonstrative
12. interrogative
13. demonstrative
14. interrogative
15. demonstrative
16. compound personal
17. demonstrative
18. demonstrative
19. compound personal

Lesson 29

Answers may vary.

Midori wanted to try sea kayaking. She called Kiera, Ramón, and Ashley and invited them to come with her. On Saturday, they all went to the beach and met the kayaking instructor, Ben. He showed them all how to paddle the kayaks. Kiera asked Ben what she should do if the kayak capsized. He explained that sea kayaks are very stable, but he said they should know what to do if one did capsize. He then demonstrated how to swim out from under a kayak and turn it upright. After that, Midori, Ashley, Kiera, and Ramón put on life jackets and set out to explore the bay. Ashley saw a sea otter and pointed it out to Ramón. He said that he had never seen a sea otter before. Midori gasped when a harbor seal swam right past Kiera and her. Kiera reminded Ashley, Ramón, and Midori that they should all make sure not to disturb any wildlife swimming near them. Synonym Watch: drudgery—toil

Lesson 30

PART I

1. <u>have</u> you heard of a physicist named <u>dr.</u> <u>stephen</u> <u>hawking</u>?
2. <u>isn't</u> he a professor at <u>cambridge</u> <u>university</u>?
3. <u>yes</u>, he is a professor of mathematics there.
4. <u>wasn't</u> his post once held by <u>albert</u> <u>einstein</u>?
5. <u>no</u>, it was held by <u>sir</u> <u>isaac</u> <u>newton</u>.
6. <u>doesn't</u> <u>dr.</u> <u>hawking</u> study black holes in space?
7. <u>yes</u>, he wrote a best-selling book on that topic.
8. <u>am</u> <u>i</u> correct that <u>dr.</u> <u>hawking</u> is <u>british</u>?
9. <u>yes</u>, he was born in <u>oxford</u>, <u>england</u>, on <u>january</u> 8, 1942.
10. <u>did</u> you know that he was born exactly 300 years after the death of <u>galileo</u>?
11. <u>hawking</u> received his doctorate from <u>cambridge</u> <u>university</u> in 1966.

PART II

12. Doesn't Stephen Hawking have a disease of the nervous system?
13. Yes, it is called amyotrophic lateral sclerosis.
14. A famous baseball player was also afflicted with this disease.
15. His name was Lou Gehrig, and he played for the New York Yankees.
16. Is it true that Dr. Hawking cannot speak, walk, or move more than a few muscles?
17. Yes, but he uses technology effectively to communicate.

Lesson 31

PART I

1. "<u>you've</u> got to be crazy to want to work on a tanker!" bellowed the captain.
2. Farid said, "<u>i've</u> worked on tankers before."
3. The captain told Farid that the run from Valdez, Alaska, to Los Angeles was no piece of cake.
4. "<u>i</u> know it is long and dangerous," said Farid.
5. "<u>tanker</u> explosions happen all too often," said the captain.
6. Then he looked up and said that it was just about to rain.
7. "<u>where's</u> the foul-weather gear?" asked Farid.
8. The captain told Farid that he should see Ms. Townsend, the chief mate.
9. "<u>i</u> bet this ship is six hundred feet long," Farid said to himself.
10. The chief mate said that Farid's gear was in a locker.
11. Farid asked if anyone was going ashore after dinner.
12. The mate said, "<u>i</u> think everyone will stay aboard."
13. "<u>we'll</u> be loading liquid tallow tonight," she continued.
14. "<u>can't</u> the night mate handle that?" asked Farid.
15. Ms. Townsend explained that it was important to have the crew on board in case any problems developed.
16. Farid said, "<u>i'll</u> be staying aboard, too."
17. He said that he would be writing letters to his family.

PART II

Answers will vary.

Lesson 33

PARTS I AND II

Answers will vary.

PART III

5. Mel asked, "Doesn't your vacation begin this month?"
6. "Yes, and soon I'll be in Chadron, Nebraska," Debra replied.

PARTS IV AND V

Answers will vary.

Lesson 34

PART I

1. You, may have heard, story
2. person, discovered, cave
3. he, was emptying, traps
4. He, saw, opening
5. curiosity, lured, him
6. he, found, formations
7. Miles, caverns, were discovered
8. Floyd Collins, explored, mapped, cave
9. He, would take, lanterns, food
10. he was seeking, entrance
11. He, entered, passageway
12. Neighbors, rescuers, could save, him
13. people, named, cave
14. tourists, visit, Floyd Collins Crystal Cave

PART II

Answers will vary.
Antonym Watch: inept—capable

Lesson 35

PART I

1. deferred
2. denounce
3. dental
4. dragged
5. dreamed
6. error
7. fable
8. fenced
9. file
10. fussing

PART II

11. X
12. mer-ry
13 fin-ish
14. X
15. X
16. giv-en
17. X
18. sup-ply
19. X
20. writ-ten
21. fu-el
22. sel-dom
23. swag-ger
24. be-tray
25. stir-ring
26. de-ny
27. X
28. X
29. win-try
30. X

Word Whiz: rectify, rectangle, rectory

Lesson 36

PART I

1. several
2. answered
3. hundred
4. always
5. absence
6. deceive
7. arctic
8. athlete
9. truly
10. ceiling
11. because
12. friend
13. government
14. having
15. foreign
16. writing

PART II

17. sin-cere
18. piz-za
19. de-part-ment
20. stran-ger
21. ter-min-al
22. an-gel-ic
23. def-i-nite
24. de-scribe
25. du-ra-tion
26. sat-is-fy
27. e-con-o-my
28. trag-e-dy

PART III

Answers may vary.
Respellings should match those in the dictionary used.
Word Whiz: misinformed, mismatched, mislabeled

Lesson 37

PART I

1. high, plains; silvery, sage
2. Huge, mountains; rocky, mountains; clear, lakes; cold, lakes
3. many, streams; swift, streams; clear, streams
4. Eager, anglers; long, distances
5. deep, ruts; wooden, wheels
6. hopeful, prospectors; dusty, trails
7. tall, Pedro Altube; great, herds
8. This, settler; early, settler; largest, ranch

PART II

Answers will vary.

Lesson 38

PART I

1. world's, ship; its, owners
2. its, voyage; iceberg's, side
3. collision's, impact; hull's, compartments
4. their, lives; North Atlantic's, depths
5. disaster's, toll
6. *Titanic's*, passengers; its, lifeboats
7. *Titanic's*, tragedy; passengers' safety
8. his, spot; her, spot
9. their, versions; night's, events
10. James Cameron's, movie; my, favorite

Lesson 39

PART I

Adjectives

lonely	Every	four	unknown
pleasant	huge	tall	That
heavy	wet	these	piercing
last	golden	light	long
clean	pleasant	high	damp
pale	damp	whining	
golden	bright	unearthly	
soggy	insistent	some	

PART II

Answers will vary.

Lesson 40

PART I

1. lies
2. lie
3. laid
4. lay
5. laid
6. lay
7. lay
8. laid
9. Lie
10. lie
11. laid
12. lying

PART II

Answers may vary.

13. lay
14. lain
15. laid
16. lay
17. lie
18. lie

Lesson 41

PART I

1. I
2. us
3. him, me
4. us
5. They
6. himself
7. I, him, them
8. she
9. she
10. they
11. us
12. me
13. she
14. her, him
15. themselves
16. We
17. us
18. we

PART II

Answers will vary.
Odd Word Out: *palette* does not belong; other words could fit in the category "track and field" or "sports equipment"; *palette* could fit in the category "materials for oil painting"

Lesson 42

PART I

1. seen
2. begun
3. given
4. came
5. did
6. seen
7. drawn
8. took
9. grown
10. run
11. flown
12. wrote
13. seen
14. flew
15. done
16. spoken
17. did

Lesson 44

PART I

1. ga-ble
2. dress-ing
3. ro-bot
4. bea-ker
5. tal-ent
6. pud-dle

PARTS II-IV

Answers will vary.

Lesson 45

PART I

1. it's
2. he'd
3. he'd
4. who's
5. there's
6. you're
7. they're
8. what's

PART II

9. It's
10. Its
11. It's
12. You're
13. They're
14. their
15. They're
16. its
17. who's
18. You're
19. your
20. Whose

Name That Job: aircraft pilot. Paragraphs will vary.

Lesson 46

PART I

1. anywhere; will grow
2. rapidly; grow
3. usually; require
4. sometimes; grow
5. normally; will choose
6. indoors; can be started
7. carefully; must prepare
8. usually; can buy
9. commonly; is used
10. nearby; need
11. cautiously; should water
12. easily; may be drowned
13. usually; is rewarded
14. Soon; will enjoy

PART II

Answers will vary.
Word Whiz: implement, compliment, supplement

Lesson 47

PART I

1. few, adjective
2. always, adverb
3. important, adjective
4. remarkable, adjective
5. often, adverb
6. famous, adjective
7. few, adjective

8. everywhere, adverb
9. famous, adjective
10. intelligent, adjective
11. effective, adjective
12. fine, adjective
13. seldom, adverb
14. famous, adjective

PART II

Answers will vary.

Lesson 48

1. <u>still</u>; is played; verb
2. <u>even</u>; wrote; verb
3. <u>extremely</u>; crowded; adjective
4. <u>unusually</u>; late; adjective
5. <u>immediately</u>; became; verb
6. <u>seriously</u>; studied; verb
7. <u>very</u>; first; adjective
8. <u>sometimes</u>; doubted; verb
9. <u>truly</u>; successful; adjective
10. <u>very</u>; big; adjective

Word Whiz: confident, incident, resident, accident, president

Lesson 49

PART I

1. unusual, <u>group</u>; unusually, <u>poorly</u>
2. good, <u>seats</u>; well, <u>did carry</u>
3. really, <u>had expected</u>; real, <u>treat</u>
4. great, <u>conductor</u>; greatly, <u>impress</u>
5. melodic, <u>music</u>; melodically, <u>was played</u>
6. clearly, <u>had</u>; clear, <u>grasp</u>
7. loud, <u>parts</u>: loudly, <u>were played</u>
8. soft, <u>parts</u>; softly, <u>were played</u>
9. near, <u>sat</u>; nearly, <u>had</u>
10. quiet, <u>amazement</u>; quietly, <u>left</u>

PART II

Answers will vary.
Name That Job: drummer; paragraphs will vary; check to be sure they are accurate.

Lesson 50

PART I

1. <u>what</u> is especially notable about the <u>nile</u>, the <u>amazon</u>, and the <u>yangtze</u>?
2. <u>they</u> are the three longest rivers in the world.
3. <u>the mississippi</u> and the <u>missouri</u> are also rivers of considerable length.
4. <u>did</u> you know that the cities with the coldest average temperatures are in <u>asia</u>?
5. <u>many</u> of the warmest cities are in <u>africa</u> or <u>india</u>.
6. <u>the</u> hottest city in all of <u>africa</u> is probably <u>timbuktu</u>.

7. <u>several south american</u> capital cities are at high altitudes.
8. <u>lhasa</u>, the capital city of <u>tibet</u>, lies northeast of <u>mount everest</u>.
9. <u>what</u> do <u>los angeles</u>, <u>california</u>, and <u>delhi</u>, <u>india</u>, have in common?
10. <u>both</u> of these metropolitan areas have more than ten million residents.

PART II

11. Mary asked, "Why are you interested in facts about the world, Peter?"
12. "I am interested in these facts for several reasons," Peter replied.
13. "You see, Mary, I want to travel around the world someday," he continued.
14. "What would it be like to live in the Andes?" he asked.
15. Mary said, "I would like to visit Addis Ababa, the capital of Ethiopia."
16. "Have you had a chance to try Ethiopian food?" she asked.

Lesson 51

1. here, of
2. like
3. of
4. at
5. got
6. like, long
7. go, and
8. like
9. got
10. she, went, and
11. to
12. on, at
13. he
14. here, they
15. like
16. went, and

17. That was fascinating, but I still don't know where the supermarket gets its bananas.
18. Most of the bananas we eat in this country are imported from Central America.

Lesson 52

PART I

1. Your
2. Carl and me
3. It's
4. your
5. himself
6. themselves
7. Whose
8. himself
9. You're
10. They're
11. Their
12. they're
13. It's
14. its
15. its
16. their
17. himself

PART II

18. your
19. their
20. my

Matching Meanings: infer—conclude; imply—suggest; reply—answer; sentences will vary; check to be sure that *infer, imply,* and *reply* are used correctly.

Lesson 53

PART I

1. May	4. wrote	7. set	10. lie
2. can	5. teach	8. taught	11. set
3. made	6. sat	9. may	12. learn

PART II

13. drew	17. saw
14. thrown	18. set
15. bought	19. wrote
16. written	20. written

Synonym Watch: fanciful—imaginative

Lesson 55

PARTS I–III

Answers will vary.

Lesson 56

PART I

1. of wood, piece
2. of clay, foundation
3. in her model, beams
4. of the model, inch
5. from a doctor, depressors
6. of great strength, Glue
7. for the floor, joists
8. of flat sticks, floor
9. between the rafters, matchbooks
10. with realistic details, model
11. about construction, lessons

PART II

Answers will vary.

Lesson 57

PART I

1. at the damage, looked
2. on the hill, had failed
3. by the truck, had been smashed
4. from the truck, had leaped
5. with the emergency brake, had slowed
6. in the truck's path, had been standing
7. on the pavement, was scattered
8. by that truck, was hit
9. on the far sidewalk, were walking
10. With great skill, had prevented
11. to its safety check, had been driving

PART II

Answers will vary.
Connecting Meanings: rotund—round; lenient—not
strict; fervent—passionate

Lesson 58

PART I

1. recipe of his own, adjective
2. dumped into a big mixer, adverb
3. flour of whole grains, adjective
4. added during the mixing, adverb
5. Nuts in bread dough, adjective
6. texture of the dough, adjective
7. used as a sweetener, adverb
8. kneaded on a floured board, adverb
9. added to the mix, adverb
10. mounds of dough, adjective
11. baked in the large oven, adverb
12. aroma of his bread, adjective

PART II

Answers will vary.
Synonym Watch: tepid—lukewarm

Lesson 59

PART I

1. in	5. in	9. off	13. off
2 Among	6. of	10. between	14. in
3. from	7. between	11. in	
4. among	8. from	12. into	

PART II

Answers will vary.

Lesson 60

PART I

1. she, go	8. like, at
2. like	9. here, like
3. went, and	10. of
4. they	11. there
5. she	12. at
6. at	13. got, like
7. went, and	14. she, went, and

PART II

15. any	20. ever	25. those
16. any	21. aren't	26. ever
17. an	22. Those	27. threw
18. should	23. ever	28. should not
19. should have	24. have	

Lesson 61

PART I

1. creamy	9. disgustingly
2. fresh	10. hoarse
3. really	11. pretty
4. good	12. great

5. noisily
6. bad
7. brave
8. well, softly

13. proudly
14. very
15. good

PART II

Answers will vary.

Lesson 62

PART I

1. plant
2. rainforest
3. rare
4. vine

5. wider
6. fleshy
7. red
8. beautiful

9. terrible
10. scent
11. good
12. pollinators

13. size
14. rotten
15. food
16. distributors

PART II

Answers will vary.
Word Whiz: deceit, conceit, receipt

Lesson 63

PART I

1. (pablo) told (maisha) about a movie review he had just read.
2. "(did) you read it on the Internet?" (maisha) asked.
3. "(yes)(i) found it on a Web site that reprints movie reviews," (pablo) replied.
4. (he) said that the review praised a new movie called (snow falling on cedars)
5. "(is) it based on the book by (david guterson)?" asked (maisha)
6. "(yes) and a young actor, (rick yune) is one of the stars," (pablo) said.
7. (then)(pablo) said that (youki kidou) (ethan hawke) (sam shepard) and (james cromwell) also appear in the film.
8. (maisha) recalled that (james cromwell) had been nominated for an Academy Award for his performance in the movie called (babe)
9. (pablo) then said that (sam shepard) was an Academy Award nominee for his performance in the movie entitled (the right stuff)

PART II

10. "Who directed <u>Snow Falling on Cedars</u>?" Maisha asked.
11. Pablo said that Scott Hicks was the director.
12. Pablo explained that Hicks had directed the movie called <u>Shine</u>.
13. "Where was <u>Snow Falling on Cedars</u> shot?" asked Maisha.
14. "Much of the movie was filmed in British Columbia, the westernmost province in Canada," Pablo said.
15. "Usually I only like comedies, but I think I'll go to see <u>Snow Falling on Cedars</u>," Maisha said.

Lesson 64

Answers may vary.

I heard a sad story from a family I know. One day a person came to their house and talked them into buying a new furnace. Between you and me, they aren't always very careful, and they signed the contract without reading it.

They felt good about having bought the furnace until the workers installed it. The price of that furnace was nearly $6,000. It took all the money they had in the bank to pay for it. The people in that family felt like lying down and crying.

They felt they couldn't afford a lawyer, so they paid those people. Now the cold weather has come, and the furnace doesn't work properly. The company that sold them the furnace has disappeared.

Those people learned a hard lesson. Don't ever sign anything unless you're sure of what it says. Be very careful, too, about buying things from people who come to your door without an invitation.

Lesson 66

PARTS I AND II

Answers will vary.

PART III

Sentences will vary.
7. January 3, 1998   8. Dublin, New Hampshire
(A comma follows the year and the state unless they end the sentence.)

PART IV

Answers will vary.

Lesson 67

PART I

Answers may vary.
1. Guavas and mangoes grow in the tropics.
2. They can't be grown in North Dakota because they need warmth all year.
3. When they are ripe, bananas are tasty fruits.
4. Many residents of the United States eat pineapples, but few have seen a zapote.
5. This fruit can't be picked until it is ripe.
6. I'll serve either pineapple jam or guava jelly.
7. I eat avocados when I visit my friends in Mazatlán.

PART II

Answers may vary.

8. Hi	10. Sorry	12. Help
9. Ouch	11. Hurry	13. Horrors

Lesson 68

PART I

1. (eat), ate, eaten, eating
2. go, went, (gone), going
3. lay, (laid), laid, laying
4. (hear), heard, heard, hearing
5. drag, dragged, dragged, (dragging)
6. set, set, (set), setting
7. bring, (brought), brought, bringing
8. buy, bought, bought, (buying)
9. tear, tore, (torn), tearing
10. teach, taught, taught, (teaching)

PART II

11. given	14. lying	17. written
12. sat	15. called	18. did
13. wrote	16. take	

Lesson 69

PART I

1. strapped	5. flared	9. relaxed
2. flashed	6. slammed	10. fell
3. made	7. catches	
4. will destroy	8. faded	

PART II

Answers will vary.
Odd Word Out: *physicist* does not belong; other words could fit in the category "doctors who treat mental and emotional problems"; *physicist* could fit in the category "physical scientists."

Lesson 70

PART I

1. <u>will have reached</u>, future perfect
2. <u>will have created</u>, future perfect
3. <u>have been</u>, present perfect
4. <u>have hit</u>, present perfect
5. <u>had been lost</u>, past perfect
6. <u>will have been tamed</u>, future perfect
7. <u>have estimated</u>, present perfect
8. <u>has produced</u>, present perfect
9. <u>have protested</u>, present perfect
10. <u>will have forced</u>, future perfect
11. <u>had built</u>, past perfect
12. <u>will have been submerged</u>, future perfect
13. <u>have studied</u>, present perfect
14. <u>will have studied</u>, future perfect

PART II

Answers may vary.
Near Misses: Second sentence: *curator* should be *curative*.

Lesson 71

PART I

1. go, plural	8. is, singular
2. am, singular	9. are, plural
3. want, plural	10. come, plural
4. have, plural	11. sells, singular
5. are, plural	12. tells, singular
6. is, singular	13. come, plural
7. has, singular	

PART II

14. catches	16. sits	18. is
15. Were	17. point	

Lesson 72

PART I

1. work	5. write	9. sell	13. have
2. are	6. are	10. are	14. see
3. create	7. makes	11. own	
4. designs	8. are	12. support	

PART II

15. were	18. Were	21. spoil
16. Is	19. are	22. isn't
17. sit	20. are	

Lesson 73

PART I

1. run-on	5. run-on
2. comma splice	6. fragment
3. fragment	7. run-on
4. fragment	8. comma splice

PART II

(Sentences may vary; some possibilities are below.)

9. The Ediacarans were soft-bodied creatures, and they lived in ancient seas.
10. When scientists first studied these strange creatures in the 1940s and '50s, the Ediacarans were classified as ancestors of modern sea animals.
11. But now, scientists are having second thoughts about some Ediacarans' classification.
12. Some Ediacarans had no legs, no mouths, no digestive tracts.
13. Because they were too different from modern animals, the two groups could not be related.
14. They might have been immobile, jelly-filled organisms with quilted bodies.
15. These Ediacarans may have been plants, or they may have been something entirely different.
16. These ancient creatures were bizarre, and alien life forms might resemble them.

Connecting Meanings: expensive—costly; pensive—thinking deeply; apprehensive—uneasy

Lesson 74

PART I

1. "<u>hugh</u>, you look like some weird insect!" shouted <u>terry</u>.
2. <u>hugh</u> asked, "<u>haven't</u> you ever seen a gas mask before?"
3. "<u>no</u>, <u>i've</u> only seen pictures of them," <u>terry</u> replied.
4. "<u>but</u> <u>i</u> do know who invented the gas mask," she said.
5. "<u>garrett</u> <u>a. morgan</u> was the inventor," she continued.
6. "<u>was</u> he a resident of the <u>united states</u>, <u>terry</u>?" <u>hugh</u> asked.
7. "<u>yes</u>, <u>mr. morgan</u> was born on <u>march</u> 4, 1877, in <u>paris</u>, <u>kentucky</u>," she said.
8. "<u>his</u> ancestors were from <u>europe</u>, <u>africa</u>, and <u>north america</u>," <u>terry</u> continued.
9. "<u>terry</u>, how do you know so much about <u>garrett morgan</u>?" <u>hugh</u> asked.
10. <u>terry</u> answered, "<u>i'm</u> doing research on <u>american</u> inventors."

PART II

11. "I've also learned a lot about Thomas A. Edison and Elias Howe, two other famous inventors," she said.
12. Then she said, "Morgan came to Cleveland, Ohio, in 1895 with just ten cents in his pocket."
13. "He must have worked, saved, and developed his talents," Hugh guessed.
14. "Yes, Morgan opened a tailoring shop in 1909," Terry replied.
15. "How can you know so much and not recognize one of Morgan's greatest inventions?" Hugh asked.

Odd Word Out: *botany* does not belong; other words could fit in the category "doctors' specialties" or "kinds of medical practice"; *botany* could fit in the category "life sciences."

Lesson 75

PART I

1. have
2. found
3. looks
4. sat
5. buzzes
6. saw, were
7. pretend
8. has
9. goes
10. look
11. does
12. eat
13. stung
14. are
15. saves

PART II

16. <u>have</u>, present
17. <u>have mistaken</u>, present perfect
18. <u>read</u>, past
19. <u>has</u>, present
20. <u>will learn</u>, future
21. <u>had seen</u>, past perfect
22. <u>will spot</u>, future
23. <u>will have made</u>, future perfect
24. <u>have kept</u>, present perfect

Lesson 77

PART I

Answers will vary.

PART II

Sentences will vary.
5. will say
6. had learned
7. take(s)
8. will have gone
9. spoke
10. (have *or* has) given

PART III

Answers will vary.

Lesson 78

PART I

1. <u>permit</u>
2. <u>industrious</u>
3. <u>peacefully</u>
4. <u>within</u>
5. <u>level</u>
6. <u>joy</u>
7. <u>hinder</u>
8. <u>few</u>
9. <u>modest</u>
10. <u>repel</u>
11. <u>defeat</u>
12. <u>frown</u>

PART II

Answers may vary.
13. above, under
14. always, never
15. happy, sad
16. dawn, sunset
17. loud, quiet
18. courageous, cowardly
19. quiet, stormy
20. correct, wrong
21. closing, opening
22. careful, careless

Lesson 79

PART I

1. "Two-person volleyball," said Margharita, "is an extremely fast game."
2. "Soon," Lin said eagerly, "Margharita and I will compete in a tournament."
3. Margharita told Lin, "Yesterday our coach shouted, 'That was your best practice ever!'"
4. "What," asked Alice, "is the greatest challenge to overcome in two-person volleyball?"
5. "Selfish players," Margharita said with a glance at Tammy, "usually don't do well in this game."
6. Lin said, "We support each other by saying things like, 'Good serve!'"
7. Margharita added, "A famous volleyball player once said, 'Know your partner's abilities well.'"
8. "I hear what you're saying," said Alice, "but don't you two ever feel competitive toward one another?"
9. Lin explained, "Our coach put it best when he said, 'There's no time for rivalry on the court.'"
10. "So," said Alice, "when do you hit the beach for the tournament?"
11. "It's coming up," Margharita said, "the first week in June!"

PART II

Answers will vary.

Lesson 80

PART I

1. bear
2. great
3. hair
4. soul
5. flair
6. steak
7. sale
8. see
9. so (sow)
10. read
11. stair
12. sent

PART II

Sentences will vary.
13. hour
14. no
15. threw
16. two, too
17. road, rode
18. flower
19. one
20. buy
21. who's
22. their, they're
23. you're
24. its

Lesson 81

1. noun	7. pronoun	13. verb
2. preposition	8. conjunction	14. noun
3. adverb	9. adverb	15. interjection
4. noun	10. adjective	16. noun
5. verb	11. conjunction	17. verb
6. adjective	12. adverb	

Connecting Meanings: detract—take away from, deter—discourage, detest—hate; sentences will vary; make sure that *detract, deter,* and *detest* are used correctly.

Lesson 82

1. <u>books</u>, <u>articles</u>; <u>have been written</u>; (no direct object)
2. <u>People</u>; <u>mistake</u>; things
3. <u>gas</u>; <u>has fooled</u>; people
4. <u>Aircraft</u>, <u>balloons</u>; <u>account</u>; (no direct object)
5. <u>people</u>; <u>have taken</u>; pictures
6. <u>Some</u>; <u>have</u>; explanation
7. <u>few</u>; <u>show</u>; objects
8. <u>These</u>; <u>hover</u>, <u>soar</u>; (no direct object)
9. <u>kinds</u>; <u>have taken</u>; pictures
10. <u>list</u>; <u>includes</u>; doctors, police officers, teachers
11. <u>Many</u>; <u>sign</u>; statements
12. <u>They</u>; <u>describe</u>; experiences
13. <u>organizations</u>; <u>collect</u>; statements
14. <u>people</u>; <u>have made</u>; statements
15. <u>Jimmy Carter</u>; <u>saw</u>; UFO

Synonym Watch: lethal—deadly

Lesson 83

PART I

1. better	7. bigger	13. tallest
2. best	8. heaviest	14. taller
3. more loyal	9. smaller	15. quietest
4. most developed	10. tiniest	16. highest
5. more sensitive	11. shorter	17. curlier
6. keener	12. smallest	18. most popular

PART II

Sentences will vary.
19. larger   20. most beautiful

Lesson 84

Answers will vary.
Antonym Watch: insert—extract

Lesson 85

Answers will vary.

Lesson 86

Answers may vary.

Two weeks ago, Will and I decided to attend this year's sports and boat show. The producers were charging ten dollars per ticket for admission. Since Will works near the ticket agency, I gave him money to buy a ticket for me. When Friday came, Will didn't call me or bring me a ticket. I had begun to miss those ten dollars, because I didn't have any more money. I decided to see Will himself and get that money back.

When I reached Will's building and walked into his cluttered apartment, I immediately saw that he was very sick. His face was pale, and he was lying on the couch. He said he was sorry that he hadn't been able to buy tickets for him and me. I sat down and told him I was sorry that he was sick. Both of us guys were sorry, but whose money was missing?

He asked me to grab his wallet off the table. I'm no fool, so I did it without hesitation. He dug out ten dollars and gave them to me. At least one of us couldn't have felt better.

Lesson 88

541 W. Main St.
Dayton, OH 45401
September 25, 1999

Mr. T. J. Monroe
Office Manager
Skelton and Inai Advertising
7921 Hill Dr.
Dayton, OH 45401

Dear Mr. Monroe:

My friend Lita Bautista, an employee of your firm, has told me that you have an opening for a mail clerk. I am very interested in beginning a career in advertising. I would welcome an opportunity to work as your mail clerk while learning about this fascinating field. I have enclosed my résumé, and I will call you on Monday to ask to schedule an interview.

Yours truly,
Marjorie Allen

Lesson 89

PART I

1. no	6. no	11. yes (.)
2. yes (.)	7. yes (?)	12. yes (?)
3. yes (!)	8. yes (.)	13. no
4. no	9. no	14. yes (.)
5. yes (.)	10. no	15. no

PART II

Answers will vary.
Optional Exercise:

2. declarative	8. declarative
3. exclamatory	11. declarative
5. declarative	12. interrogative
7. interrogative	14. declarative

Lesson 90

PART I

1. I; I	3. <u>Henson</u>; Henson
2. <u>The article</u>; article	4. <u>He</u>; He

5. He and his parents; He, parents
6. Young Henson; Henson
7. Several years at sea and many adventures; years, adventures
8. the young sailor; sailor
9. he and a young naval officer; he, officer
10. The officer's name; name

PART II

11. joined Peary on all his Arctic expeditions after 1891; Peary
12. were heading for the North Pole in 1908 (no direct object)
13. spoke the Inuit language; language
14. obtained the supplies and trained the dogs; supplies, dogs
15. accompanied them on the journey's last stage; them
16. were Coqueeh, Ootah, Eginwah, and Seegloo (no direct object)
17. halted Peary near the North Pole; Peary
18. sent his assistant on without him; assistant
19. reached the North Pole first; North Pole
20. joined him about an hour later; him
21. planted the American flag at the Pole on April 6, 1909; flag

Lesson 91

PART I

1. towers
2. hutches
3. shelves
4. parties
5. chimneys
6. women

PART II

7. forest's   forests'
8. wolf's   wolves'
9. child's   children's
10. sentry's   sentries'
11. monkey's   monkeys'
12. coach's   coaches'

PART III

13. She and I
14. she
15. us
16. We
17. me
18. Whose
19. me
20. me
21. themselves
22. They
23. You're
24. Your
25. its

Lesson 92

PART I

1. changes
2. was
3. have changed
4. have
5. have entered
6. began
7. conquered
8. call
9. had spoken
10. spoke
11. mixed
12. will continue
13. will have added
14. will develop

PART II

Answers will vary. Possible answers are as follows:
15. changes; have; call
16. was; began; conquered; spoke; mixed
17. will continue; will develop
18. have changed; have entered
19. had spoken
20. will have added

Odd Word Out: *Linguini* does not belong. Other words could fit into the category "terms used to talk about language." *Linguini* could fit into the category "types of pasta."

Lesson 93

PART I

1. often; almost; human
2. real; this; artificial; yet
3. Still; more; more; today
4. dangerous; unpleasant; impossible
5. robotic; safely; Alaskan
6. This; spidery; eight
7. famous; harsh; rocky
8. more; ordinary; daily
9. Innovative; now; very; small
10. miniature; together

PART II

Answers will vary.
Connecting Meanings: perpetrate—bring about; perpetuate—make last; perplex—confuse

Lesson 94

PART I

1. in all advertisements, adverb
2. to our emotions, adverb
3. of fairness, adjective
4. for car safety features, adjective
5. of serious accidents, adjective
6. of this nation, adjective
7. by one hundred million people, adverb
8. on daytime TV, adjective
9. during Saturday morning cartoon shows, adverb
10. with the most entertaining ads, adjective
11. after midnight, adjective
12. at three A.M., adverb
13. during prime time, adjective
14. during the Super Bowl, adjective
15. during commute hours, adverb
16. in their cars, adjective

PART II

Answers will vary.

Lesson 95

Answers will vary.

Lesson 96

PART I

1. ras shamra was once an important phoenician city.
2. the city, a port on the mediterranean sea, was formerly named ugarit.
3. great discoveries at ras shamra were made by french scientists.
4. an american professor also made a sensational discovery.
5. professor anne d. kilmer found possibly the world's oldest song.

6. the ugarits wrote in the hurrian language.
7. professor kilmer discovered that they wrote music, poems, and stories.
8. the ugaritic music was played at the university of california in 1974.
9. the audience may have heard the sound of history's oldest written music.
10. professor kilmer's discovery changed many people's ideas about the development of music.

PART II

11. Homer's poetic story about the fall of the ancient city of Troy is called *The Iliad*.
12. "Isn't your friend Rose studying Homer's work?" asked Fred.
13. "Yes, and she is giving a report on it tomorrow," I answered.
14. "Do people still believe that the story of the Trojan War was just a Greek myth?" asked Fred.
15. "Myth and fact in ancient writing are usually very hard to separate," I replied.

Connecting Meanings: ballad–song; ballot–form for voting; ballet–graceful type of dance

Lesson 97

PART I

1. May	4. learned	7. set	10. lie
2. can	5. set	8. lain	
3. taught	6. can	9. lay	

PART II

Answers may vary.

11. Because I camp far off the main trails, I always carry a compass.
12. I never leave trash along the trail.
13. Hikers have to get permits to camp in the wilderness.
14. That campfire is still smoldering and could start a forest fire.
15. The people who built it should have poured more water on it.
16. Do you know where the creek is?

Lesson 98

PARTS I–II

Answers will vary.

PART III

Sentences will vary.

8. begin(s)	10. will drive	12. had ridden
9. broke	11. (have *or* has) gone	13. will have known

PART IV

20. among	21. from	22. into

PARTS V AND VI

Answers will vary.

INDEX OF TOPICS FEATURED IN LEVEL III
(Numbers listed are page numbers.)